ALSO BY G. BRUCE KNECHT

The Proving Ground:
The Inside Story of the 1998 Sydney to Hobart Race

Hooked:
Pirates, Poaching, and the Perfect Fish

Simon & Schuster
1230 Avenue of the Americas
New York, NY 10020

First Simon & Schuster hardcover edition March 2013

SIMON & SCHUSTER and colophon are registered trademarks of Simon & Schuster, Inc.

For information about special discounts for bulk purchases, please contact Simon & Schuster Special Sales at 1-866-506-1949 or business@simonandschuster.com.

The Simon & Schuster Speakers Bureau can bring authors to your live event. For more information or to book an event, contact the Simon & Schuster Speakers Bureau at 1-866-248-3049 or visit our website at www.simonspeakers.com.

Designed by Katy Riegel

Manufactured in the United States of America

1 3 5 7 9 10 8 6 4 2

Library of Congress Cataloging-in-Publication Data
Knecht, G. Bruce.
Grand ambition: an extraordinary yacht, the people who built it, and the millionaire who can't really afford it / G. Bruce Knecht.
p. cm.
Includes bibliographical references and index.
1. Lady Linda (Yacht). 2. Yachting—United States—Biography. 3. Yacht building—United States—History. 4. Von Allmen, Doug. 5. Capitalists and financiers—Florida—Biography. 6. Venture capital—United States—Biography. 7. Trinity Yachts (Firm). 8. Boatbuilding—Mississippi. 9. Boatbuilders—Mississippi—Biography. 10. Boating industry—United States—Biography. I. Title.
GV815.K63 2013
797.1246—dc23   2012030486

ISBN 978-1-4165-7600-6
ISBN 978-1-4165-7628-0 (ebook)

GRAND AMBITION

An Extraordinary Yacht, the People Who Built It, and the Millionaire Who Can't Really Afford It

G. Bruce Knecht

SIMON & SCHUSTER

New York   London   Toronto   Sydney   New Delhi

For Andrew

Contents

Prologue

THE ALARM clock next to Gale Tribble's bed came alive with a blast of country music at 4:15 a.m. An ashtray holding the remains of the previous night's final cigarette was balancing on top of the clock, so he was careful as he reached to turn off the radio. Then came a more insistent alarm, his cell phone, programmed to ring at 4:16. Hoisting himself from the bed, Tribble shuffled across the cluttered bedroom and opened a door that led directly into the kitchen, where he switched on a coffee machine he had loaded the night before.

It was a cold January morning, so he started to get dressed with a full-body layer of long underwear. Then jeans and a blue shirt that carried the name of his employer, Trinity Yachts, just above the left breast pocket, followed by wool socks and gray sneakers that were reinforced with steel to protect his toes. Returning to the kitchen, he reached into the refrigerator to remove a fried-egg sandwich his daughter had made, along with a Coke and a sticky bun. Once he had packed the food, his breakfast and lunch, into a cooler, Tribble filled a nonspill metal cup with coffee. His fire engine red pickup truck—a meticulously maintained eight-year-old Ford—was just a few steps away. Switching on the headlights, he commenced his twenty-mile commute by igniting a Camel Light and adjusting the volume of his radio, which was tuned to the same station as his alarm clock. He could shorten the travel time by taking the highway, but that would mean six additional miles and more gasoline, so he generally stuck to back roads.

Fifty-nine years old, Tribble is a wiry man whose five-foot-nine frame carries just 135 pounds, his weight ever since he graduated from high school. His black and silver hair is longish but neatly trimmed. His eyes are blue and deeply set, and his cheeks are also sunken, hollowed out because he had lost all his teeth many years earlier. He relies on dentures to eat.

Tribble lives in Pass Christian, Mississippi, a Gulf Coast community midway between New Orleans and Mobile, Alabama. He has never lived anywhere else, and his house, a compact, single-story, rectangular structure, is the one in which he grew up. Elevated above the ground by cinder blocks, it looks like a mobile home, but it was actually built by his father back in the 1940s. It is set on thirty-eight acres, most of which are overgrown, although Tribble had cleared out patches here and there to grow vegetables and raise chickens. He has never had much money, but his expenses are similarly modest. There is no mortgage on the house, and the annual real estate taxes are $659.

Back when he was in high school, Tribble wrote soulful songs that were inspired by the country ballads he started listening to with his parents. He also played the saxophone, and he sometimes thought about becoming a professional musician. But he ended up learning how to weld metals and went to work at the shipyard where his father had been employed for almost two decades. Tribble had been with several shipyards over the years, and he joined Trinity in 2006, not long after it moved from Hurricane Katrina–ravaged New Orleans to Gulfport, Mississippi. Forty years after he began his career, his hourly wage had gone from $2.50 to $18.50, but he said the buying power of his earnings was unchanged. "I used to be able to fill up the car with groceries for twenty dollars," he remembered, "and gas cost twenty-eight cents a gallon."

Tribble is a shipfitter. He has helped build everything from barges and oceangoing cargo vessels to naval destroyers and aircraft carriers—more than one hundred vessels in all. He has always worked in open-air sheds where the conditions are often challenging, particularly in the summer when the temperature regularly rises above 100 degrees. But he almost never complains, not about the heat or the humidity, the early mornings or the tedium of his work, not even the gum disease that, by the time he was thirty, led to the loss of his teeth and the end of his saxophone playing. It just isn't in his nature. Unlike many of his colleagues, Tribble has never seriously considered finding a different kind of job, and he was not eager to retire. "I like what I do," he said. "And what would I do if I didn't work?"

Gale Tribble, a shipyard laborer for forty of his fifty-nine years.

THAT MORNING, Tribble was about to begin the construction of *Lady Linda,* a 187-foot yacht. In a different era, this day—January 7,

2008—would have been one of special significance, witnessed by everyone who was playing a role in the massive project. But with many of the participants communicating with one another electronically from distant locations, the only people who would see the process get under way would be Tribble and another laborer, William Packer.

Lady Linda was to be one of the largest American-made yachts since the Gilded Age, a gleaming symbol of its owner's participation in a quarter century of unprecedented wealth creation. The owner, a private equity investor named Doug Von Allmen, had committed himself to its building in 2006, not long before the boom's peak. By global standards, *Lady Linda* would not be among the very largest of the burgeoning fleet of seagoing palaces, but Von Allmen had vowed that it would be the best of those made in the United States. He wanted to disprove the conventional wisdom that America did not know how to build things anymore, as well as the long-held orthodoxy that domestically built yachts are necessarily inferior to those from Europe. Nothing would be ordinary: interior walls would be made from rare species of burl wood, floors would be paved with onyx and unusual types of marble, the furniture would be bespoke, and artworks would be commissioned on the basis of the spaces they would fill.

But the creation of *Lady Linda* would be far from glamorous, and the uncertainties that lay ahead would affect hundreds of people whose lives and livelihoods were bound up in the project: Von Allmen and Tribble, as well as a former army sniper who was now working as a pipefitter, and an illegal immigrant from Honduras who would give a lustrous finish to the yacht's exterior by sheathing it with an array of poisonous compounds. For Von Allmen, *Lady Linda* was supposed to be the ultimate embodiment of his success. Instead, he would come to question whether he could actually afford to be its owner. For Tribble and many others, the impact of the changed world—and the construction itself—would be even more profound.

✶

WHEN TRIBBLE reached Gulfport, he turned onto Seaway Road, a heavily trafficked thoroughfare where the air smelled of petroleum. Signs pointed to a variety of manufacturing and distribution operations as well as A-1 Bailbonds and a prison. Trinity was the only one of Seaway Road's businesses that had a Help Wanted sign out front, evidence of the still-soaring demand for very large yachts.

Once he parked his truck, Tribble added two additional layers of clothing: Carhartt coveralls and a jacket. It was 5:35 a.m., well before the 6:00 start of his shift. After sliding his time card through a machine to register his presence, he entered a partially enclosed metal structure that covered almost a dozen acres and the bulk of Trinity's production facilities. Like everyone, Tribble called it "the yard." Eleven vessels were at various stages of development, although some of the constructions did not look like boats. One of the largest forms, an almost completed hull, was inverted. Its disconnected bow section, which was upright, stood nearby.

Tribble found his way to a jig, a 120-foot-long steel-beamed platform on which the first phases of *Lady Linda* would be built. Three feet above the floor, the jig was surrounded by piles of recently cut pieces of aluminum of various shapes and sizes.

In traditional boatbuilding, the first step would be the assembling—or laying—of the keel: the foundation upon which everything else was built. But the order of things was different at Trinity, which, like most contemporary shipbuilders, broke the fabrication process into units. In another departure from traditional boatbuilding, most of the hull would be built upside down. It was easier—and less time consuming—for laborers to work that way. Rather than having to aim their welding torches upward, they could look down at their work.

Tribble and Packer, who got to the jig a few minutes after Tribble, would start with the engine-room module, one of four large assemblies that would compose the hull. The very first piece of the puzzle was the centerboard longitudinal, a strip of aluminum that was forty-five feet long, the full length of the module, and twenty-three inches high. Like a keel, it would run along the middle of the hull; but while keels protrude from the bottom of the hull, the centerboard would be inside. (Eventually, *Lady Linda* would also have a keel, but it would be added much later.)

The first task was to erect a pair of braces that would hold the centerboard above the jig. Once that was done, Packer manipulated the controls of the overhead travel lift—a chain-bearing crane that ran on tracks ninety feet above the floor—to deliver the centerboard to the braces. Then he climbed up onto the jig and held the centerboard firmly against one of the braces. Just after ten in the morning, Tribble used a tape measure and a level to confirm that the centerboard was in the correct position. He then lowered the face mask of his helmet and joined the centerboard to one of the braces with four small welds. Once it was attached to the other brace, the next job was welding fifty-two yard-long frames to the centerboard so that they extended from it like ribs.

When a whistle sounded at four thirty to signal the end of the workday, Tribble was in an excellent mood, for two reasons. First, the satisfaction that always came from starting something new. In addition, it was Monday, the day that always ended with his favorite meal: red beans and rice. It was a southern tradition that went back to preelectricity days when laundry was done by hand, and usually on Mondays. Since the work tied women to the house, it was the best day for them to watch over a pot of simmering beans.

The product of Tribble's labor did not look like much. He and Packer had connected twenty frames to the centerboard, ten on each side. The shiny silver assembly appeared to be flimsy, more like a supersized version of a child's Erector Set than the beginnings of a 487-ton yacht that would be formed with more than thirty thousand pieces of aluminum and cost $40 million.

1

Making Plans

If a man is to be obsessed by something, I suppose a boat is as good as anything, perhaps a bit better than most.

—E. B. White

EVAN MARSHALL, one of the world's most sought-after yacht designers, was in his London office in the fall of 2006, hunched over a door-sized desk that was covered with schematic drawings of *Lady Linda*. While his iPod shuffled through a collection of more than five thousand songs, a mix of soul, jazz, and rock from the 1960s to the present, he rarely lifted his head. When he did, it was only to look at his laptop, which held electronic versions of the same plans, together with engineering specifications.

Marshall's appearance was not what most people would expect of a yacht designer. A powerfully built black man with a shaved head, he looked like an African-American Mr. Clean. *Lady Linda* was the most important project of his career. It was his biggest yacht to date, and Von Allmen's ambitious goals gave it the potential to advance the reputation of the London-based design firm Marshall founded in 1993.

He had just begun work on *Lady Linda*'s design. His head was filled with so many thoughts, he was not sure where to begin. Marshall eventually focused on the entryway, which, like the foyer of a large house, would play a crucial role in setting the overall tone. Trinity Yachts had provided a conceptual layout, but the foyer it showed was narrow and oddly shaped, lacking the symmetry and balance Marshall believed to be prerequisites for every estimable interior space.

Turning to his computer, he used his mouse to shift the position of the walls. Although he frequently complained that the design field had suffered because young designers were so dependent on computers that they did not know how to explore concepts with freehand sketches, the forty-seven-year-old Marshall relied on his laptop to expedite many phases of the process. With fingertip ease, he could reverse the direction of stairways, drop tables and couches into a room, land a helicopter on the deck, and even stretch a yacht's overall length. Down the road, computers would enable him to create three-dimensional images into which he could incorporate furniture and fabrics.

MARSHALL HAD BEEN drawing boats since he was a child growing up in New York City. His first creations depicted relatively small vessels, inspired by his family's 32-foot cabin cruiser. His father, Kenneth, a sociology professor at Columbia University who was active in the civil rights movement, loved boats, but he never had enough money to maintain his properly, so it rarely left the dock. During an outing on Evan's sixth birthday, the craft almost sank, and was sold not long after that. But boats had already taken hold of the young Marshall's imagination, and he spent much of his boyhood filling spiral notebooks with his ideas. A few years after the aborted birthday cruise, he was walking the docks of a Hudson River marina when he came across the *Highlander,* an imposing green-hulled vessel that belonged to Malcolm Forbes, the flamboyant magazine publisher.

Although he did not know it at the time, Marshall was looking at one of the best-known yachts of the day: a collaboration between Holland's Feadship, widely believed to be the world's best builder, and the foremost yacht designer, an Australian named Jon Bannenberg.

Bannenberg had transformed yacht design. Before him, hulls were invariably white or blue, and interiors were almost always paneled with dark woods. Bannenberg used light-toned woods to create more modern interiors, introduced new shapes for hulls and windows, and incorporated previously unheard-of amenities, including elevators and movie theaters. He also encouraged owners to build bigger boats. In the mid-1990s Bannenberg designed a game-changing 316-foot giant for Leslie Wexner, the retailer who founded the women's clothing chain The Limited. The yacht—Wexner named it *Limitless*—kicked off an epic nautical footrace. The next step up was *Octopus,* a 413-footer commissioned by Microsoft billionaire Paul Allen. Shortly before he died in 2002, Bannenberg designed Oracle Corporation founder Larry Ellison's 453-foot *Rising Sun,* which became the world's largest privately owned yacht.

During his examination of the *Highlander,* when Marshall managed to glimpse into its galley, he was astounded by what he saw: a pair of commercial-sized refrigerators. Since his father's cabin cruiser had only a small ice chest, the presence of the large appliances was a revelation.

Marshall's fascination with boat design began as a childhood obsession, a youthful fantasyland, but over time he began to believe it could become something more. After studying naval architecture in college, he secured a job in 1985 with Sparkman & Stephens, a legendary New York design firm. But even then Marshall knew the United States was no longer the place where the biggest and most interesting yachts were designed or built. London had become the epicenter of yacht design, mostly because Bannenberg had located his office there, as had most of his disciples and former employees—

groups that came to include almost all of the world's best-regarded designers. In 1990 Marshall went to work for one of Bannenberg's former designers. Three years later he founded his own firm.

Evan K. Marshall.

THE PLANS Marshall was developing for *Lady Linda*'s interior layout were a cornerstone of the overall design process. The conceptual layouts Trinity had provided were just a starting point. However, they would play another role in one of the great tugs-of-war that are part of the building of almost every large yacht: even though Trinity marketed itself as a builder of custom yachts, it sought to reduce its costs by encouraging a degree of standardization. It also attempted to minimize the kind of rounded shapes that are easy to draw but expensive to fabricate because of the extra manpower they require.

Labor is the predominant expense in modern-day yacht building: the aluminum or steel used to form the hull and superstructure represents less than 5 percent of the total cost. Labor accounts for two-thirds. New materials and technologies have diminished the need for many types of blue-collar labor, but this does not apply to large metal-hulled vessels. While smaller boats could be molded out of fiberglass, it is not strong enough to build larger vessels, and no one has devised a way to construct oceangoing craft that does not involve welding thousands of pieces together, one at a time. That's why Gale Tribble has never spent more than two weeks away from work except for two periods when he was laid off in the 1970s.

Since Trinity had agreed to build *Lady Linda* for a fixed price—the base amount was $37 million, though Von Allmen would eventually agree to several increases—Marshall's instinctive taste for curves would inevitably lead to conflict. The tension would be complicated further by Marshall's own interests vis-à-vis Trinity. The company had referred several clients to him, and he did not want to do anything to jeopardize that relationship, unless he had to.

Almost every decision in *Lady Linda*'s design required a trade-off. With the foyer, Marshall wanted to find a way to expand its width, but the overall breadth of the yacht could not exceed 35 feet, and giving more room to the foyer would leave less room for the staircase and the galley that probably would be located behind the stairs. Pointing to a small space next to the foyer that he originally thought would be used for electronics, Marshall said, "Maybe I can move this closet somewhere else." He also shifted the position of a powder room. With those changes, the foyer became larger and rectangular. Marshall went on to illustrate the benefits of this by adding two pairs of double doors. One would lead toward the rear, or stern, and into the main salon, which would be *Lady Linda*'s largest space. The other doors opened to the master stateroom, a suite of rooms that would include the Von Allmens' bedroom, his and her bathrooms and wardrobes, and a study.

"The symmetry of the two sets of doors is wonderful," Marshall declared. With a few more clicks and slides of his mouse, he added opening radiuses for all of the doors, which appeared as dotted lines. Consumed by his work, Marshall's pace seemed to be accelerating. "This is the fun part," he said. "Ideas are beginning to form."

I Want to Be
an Accountant

There never was a great man yet who spent all his life inland.

—*WHITE-JACKET,* HERMAN MELVILLE

SEVERAL WEEKS after Marshall began developing *Lady Linda*'s design, he went to Fort Lauderdale, Florida, to talk to Von Allmen and his wife, Linda, the yacht's namesake, about his preliminary ideas.

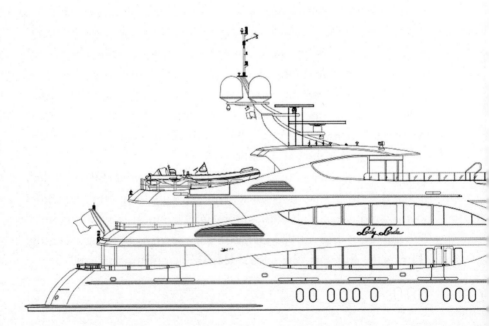

The Von Allmens' house is a sprawling Mediterranean-styled structure situated on the Intracoastal Waterway, the system of inter-connected bays and sounds that reaches from Florida to New Jersey. Opening a wrought-iron gate in front of the house, Marshall entered a small courtyard that had a gurgling fountain at the center. Through the glass of the front door, he could see the living room and, beyond that, a manicured backyard and the dock that would be home to *Lady Linda*. Linda opened the door and led Marshall to the library, where her husband was waiting. Once they sat down at a marble-topped bar, Marshall unrolled a drawing showing a side view of *Lady Linda*'s exterior. The superstructure was dominated by two long bands of continuous dark-glass windows that had swoop-ing curved shapes. The arched forms were Von Allmen's idea—he had faxed a simple sketch to Marshall several months earlier—and the designer had embraced the idea. The shapes reminded him of scimitars, and he thought they would go a long way toward estab-lishing *Lady Linda*'s character. He hoped a similar aesthetic could be carried over into the interior, with cabinetry that would be bowed rather than flat faced.

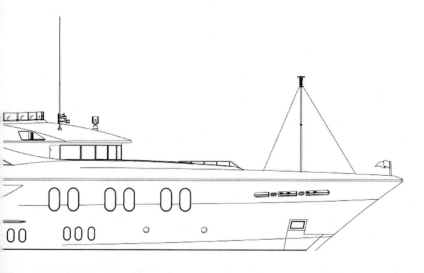

Linda obviously liked what she saw. Although she was Von Allmen's second wife, she was just a couple of years younger than her sixty-seven-year-old husband, so she did not fit the usual society page vision of a "trophy wife." She was a spirited woman who was always quick to voice her thoughts.

Von Allmen was not. For an accomplished businessman, he had always been unusually reticent. A veteran of countless negotiations, he believed that revealing too much could only impair his bargaining position. His facial expressions were also unrevealing. His most noticeable feature was his hazel eyes, which appeared to be slightly oversized, causing him to look like he was perpetually surprised. His broad face was otherwise unexpressive, as reserved as his house was dramatic.

VON ALLMEN'S reticence and perhaps his taste for very large yachts and homes were also rooted in his personal history. He had grown up in a family in which money had been an uncertain thing, and his emotions had been tethered closely to economic matters ever since. When a recession struck in the early 1980s, he fell apart completely. His first marriage and his business partnership both unraveled, and Von Allmen became so depressed that he rarely left his house. However, in the years that followed, his private equity investments and the magic-making combination of easy money, low taxes, and a surging stock market buoyed his spirits as well as his net worth.

He had come a long way. As a child growing up in Louisville, Kentucky, Von Allmen had been so physically frail that his mother did not expect him to survive, and she told him as much when he was still young. He was not interested in boats then. His main focus was cars, which was unfortunate, because his family did not own one until he was fifteen. One year after that, his father lost his job as a milkman and moved the family to Miami, where a cousin gave him a job selling reconditioned tires.

Von Allmen hated Florida. He was not interested in academics, and he had no real friends. "I always had the feeling that I was a couple of years behind everyone else," he would say many years later. After the principal told him he had missed so many days during his senior year that he could not graduate, Von Allmen stopped attending school altogether. He found a job delivering parts for an auto supply store, but his father died not long after that, and his mother decided to move back to Louisville.

Von Allmen then worked as a commercial window washer until a car accident left him unconscious. While he was still in the hospital, he vowed that he would go back to high school. Once he graduated, two years behind most of his original classmates, he went to work in a factory that made boxes; it was his job to pull cardboard containers off an assembly line and pack them together for shipping. He did not mind the work itself, but he disliked his colleagues and worried about his future. Eventually Von Allmen decided to go to college to pursue a very different kind of career path. "I want to be an accountant," he told his mother. When she asked why, he said, "Someone came to school last year and said the people who make the most money are lawyers, engineers, and accountants. I am not good enough at English to be a lawyer, and I'm not good enough at math to be an engineer, so I'm going to be an accountant."

Thanks to financial aid and money his mother borrowed from a relative, Von Allmen was able to enroll in the University of Kentucky's business college. And for the first time in his life, he was a diligent student, earning almost perfect grades. Graduating second in his class in 1965, he was hired by Peat, Marwick, Mitchell & Company to work in its Saint Louis office.

The work, auditing midsized insurance companies, was tedious, but Von Allmen's greater frustration resulted from his inability to win the respect of the partners who ran the office. Then he heard about a thirty-five-year-old Peat, Marwick client who used borrowed money to purchase a jewelry distribution business. This is when a series of life-altering lightbulbs began to turn bright in Von Allmen's mind: by buying a company of his own, he would eliminate the need to impress the bosses.

Using business directories he found in a local library, he sent letters to hundreds of company owners, asking if they might be willing to sell. In the spring of 1978, Von Allmen received an encouraging response from the owner of an Illinois company that rebuilt industrial electric motors. He agreed to sell his firm for $2 million. After a bank financed the entire cost of the acquisition, Von Allmen left Peat, Marwick and set out to improve the motor company's finances by selling off unneeded assets and trimming its operating costs. Just nine months later, he paid off the loans. By then, he had also come to another revelation: he knew less about rebuilding motors and managing a company than he did about buying businesses. So while his initial goal had been to make a single acquisition that would provide him with a stable career, he began to think more expansively: why shouldn't he spend his time buying *lots* of companies and hire other people to run them?

Over the next couple of years, Von Allmen worked with a partner from an office in Saint Louis to scour the Midwest and the South for acquisitions. By 1980, they owned six companies. All of them performed well—until the recession of 1981 and 1982, when they all ran into serious problems. That's when frictions developed in his relationships with his business partner as well as with his wife. The couple had two children: Julie, who was then thirteen, and ten-year-old David. Von Allmen soon separated from both his wife and business partner, and sold off the companies. After the proceeds were divided, he ended up with about $200,000.

Von Allmen became deeply depressed. A couple of years later, he slowly began rebuilding, personally and professionally, and he married Linda. Once the economy recovered, Von Allmen started looking for more companies to buy. Working with new partners—a former banker named Bruce Olson and Olson's wife, Kimberly—his first acquisition was a firm that sold transformers and meters to electric utilities. In his search for additional assets, Von Allmen developed a network of hundreds of small-time business brokers. Most of the opportunities they offered up were extremely small—they handled gas stations and delicatessens—but every once in a while, they represented something larger. And since the brokers were hard pressed to find investors capable of purchasing relatively big companies, Von Allmen and his partners were sometimes the only bidders.

Every one of Von Allmen's acquisitions turned out to be a profitable investment. And some were spectacular winners, such as Sunsations, a chain of 45 sunglasses stores that he and his partners snapped up for a few million dollars. They then pursued an aggressive plan to grow the business. Opening as many as four stores a week, Sunsations eventually had 350 locations and became the nation's second-largest sunglasses retailer. While Von Allmen bought businesses with the idea of keeping them for the long haul, he realized that this investment offered a special opportunity because Sunglass Hut, the field's leading retailer, was desperate to maintain its dominant position. In 1995 it paid $120 million for Sunsations, earning Von Allmen what was then the biggest payday of his career.

By then, he was spending a lot of his time in Florida. Although he had hated living there as a child, now he loved it, his thinking changed mostly because of boats. During much of his time in Saint Louis, he had a second home on the Lake of the Ozarks and acquired a series of motorboats, each one larger than the last, until he had a 43-footer. After selling Sunsations, Von Allmen bought a 55-foot motor cruiser that he kept in Florida, and a couple of years after that, he traded up to a 76-footer. Each boat whetted his appetite for more, and eventually he agreed to pay $12 million to build a 124-foot three-deck vessel.

Von Allmen said he used that yacht in an altogether different way than his previous boats: "It became a second home. When we want to change the view, we just pull up the anchor."

✫

AFTER THE Von Allmens examined Marshall's drawings of *Lady Linda*'s exterior, the conversation moved to the interior. Von Allmen was particularly eager to talk about an idea he had for the sky lounge, the space that would share the uppermost deck with the bridge, the compartment from which the yacht would be navigated. "I'd like to put the biggest flat-screen television we can find on the forward bulkhead"—the wall at the front of the room—he said. He did not explain the exact reason for his request, but it had grown out of an idea he and Linda had talked about the night before. Because the bridge would be in front of the sky lounge, there could not be any windows on that wall. Therefore, while the sky lounge would have excellent sight lines in three directions, it would be impossible to see what was directly in front of the yacht. The Von Allmens' idea was to mount a video camera at the bow that could relay the view to a large television screen. Maximizing views was always an overriding priority, and they saw no reason why they should not utilize technology to expand them. The two of them were also thinking about installing an underwater camera so they could see what was *beneath* the yacht.

Marshall promised to look into large flat-screen televisions and then brought up a different topic: the construction schedule. "I've asked Trinity for a schedule several times because we need to establish some milestones," he said, "but they haven't gotten anything back to me."

The timetable was crucial because it would figure into one of the other big battlegrounds involved in getting a big yacht built. Under Von Allmen's contract with Trinity, *Lady Linda* was supposed to be delivered to him by May 15, 2009. Every day of delay would reduce its price tag by $10,000. Given the magnitude of the potential penalty, Trinity would be inclined to pin the blame for any delay that did occur on the owner or—more likely—Marshall. This meant the milestones in Trinity's schedule might have comfortable cushions of time for the construction phases but difficult deadlines for when Marshall had to deliver various plans. Given this, he was eager to get his hands on the proposed dates so he knew exactly what he was up against.

"I've just got to get the schedule," the designer declared.

By then, Von Allmen was glancing at his watch and rising from his chair. "I know, I know," he said. "I'll call Trinity later today."

3

The Sky Is the Limit

Give us the luxuries of life, and we will dispense with its necessities.

—John Lothrop Motley,
American historian and diplomat (1814–1877)

In June 2007 the Von Allmens and several executives from Trinity Yachts were among those who traveled to Monaco, the city-state synonymous with wealth and yachting, for a glittering celebration. They gathered in the Sporting Club de Monte Carlo's ballroom—a large space best known for the way its retractable ceiling can be rolled back to reveal the sky—to honor the most noteworthy megayachts launched during the previous year. As waiters weaved through the room while balancing silver trays freighted with slender flutes of champagne, a powerful sound system pumped out the Red Hot Chili Peppers' hit song "Can't Stop."

The evening resembled the Academy Awards, or even more, the Golden Globes, with guests sitting down to several courses of food and wine before the presentation of fourteen prizes. The Von Allmens would win one for the interior design of a yacht they already owned: *Linda Lou,* a 197-footer that Lürssen, a German shipyard, had delivered to them a few months earlier. They were standing near the center of the room, chatting with several friends who had joined them on the yacht for a cruise that had taken them from Barcelona to the French Riviera before they arrived in Monaco a few days earlier.

When Von Allmen spotted John Dane III, Trinity's president and primary owner, he waved him over to talk about *Lady Linda*'s construction schedule. Von Allmen knew the $10,000-a-day delay penalty was almost impossible to enforce. Just before the party, he explained why: "Every time you make a design change, they say, 'That's going to add another two weeks to the completion date.' You can say to them, 'Hold on: you're saying that if we change one faucet, it means that it's going to hold up the whole job for two weeks?' They say, 'Yeah, well, there's a lot more involved with that faucet than you think.' So every time you sign a change order, they get another two-week extension." Von Allmen also knew Trinity was under tremendous pressure because of the number of yachts it had agreed to build and also because of its move to Gulfport, where it was struggling to reassemble its workforce.

"Listen, I know how many boats you have going," Von Allmen said to Dane, "and I don't know how you're going to do it!"

"We'll be okay—"

"I'm sure you will be, but let's come up with a schedule for my boat that's realistic, so we don't end up playing the game."

"Yeah, I know what you're saying," Dane said. "Let me take a look at it and get back to you."

THE IMPORTANCE of the awards that would be distributed reached beyond their recipients. This was reflected by the audience of more than five hundred, which included members of the megayacht economy's vast supporting cast: designers, builders, brokers, bankers, insurers, and lawyers.

Between two large round tables that were covered by royal blue tablecloths and an array of glasses, Ron Holland, a veteran designer, was marveling at the industry's globalization. He had begun his career designing small sailboats in his native New Zealand but was now based in Ireland, creating plans for vessels many times larger. One was *Mirabella V,* a 247-foot sloop that had been the world's biggest privately owned sailboat until venture capitalist Tom Perkins, who was also in the room, built an even bigger one. Holland had just returned from China, where several new yacht builders had sprung up almost overnight and where he was overseeing the construction of a 150-foot boat for a German client. "The quality of the work there is very good," he told David Ross, the president of Burger Boat Company, a builder located on the shore of Lake Michigan in Wisconsin.

Ross said the market was growing so rapidly that he was not worried about competition from China. "I was just in Dubai, where they are going to build docks for *forty thousand yachts* over the next few years," he said. "If just one percent of them are for 150-footers, we'll be in great shape. And then there's the Russians: five of the seven boats we're building right now are for Russians."

Near the back of the room, Jim Herman, an owner of an Australian yacht builder, Warren Yachts, was complaining about how the falling value of the American dollar was making it difficult to sell boats in the United States, but he was bursting with optimism nonetheless. "The industry is just exploding," he declared. "There are more orders—and the boats are getting bigger and bigger. Is it a bubble? I don't think so. I think the market is only going to get stronger."

Following dinner, Jill Bobrow, the long-time editor of *ShowBoats International,* the glossy magazine that sponsored the night's festivities, stepped onto the stage to present the awards. The first, for "Outstanding Achievement in a Motor Yacht," which was considered a lifetime-achievement award, went to *Lady Anne,* the ninth in a series of ever-larger yachts owned by Jerome Fisher.

Fisher had made his fortune after he identified a huge source of unfulfilled demand in the women's shoe market back in the 1970s: the shoes that appeared on the pages of *Vogue* and *Harper's Bazaar*— the ones the fashion czars praised and to which many women aspired—were so expensive as to be out of reach for most consumers, and there were no low-cost alternatives. Setting up manufacturing facilities in Brazil, Fisher began producing fashionable footwear at radically lower prices. He later founded Nine West, a retailer that was soon selling one out of every five pairs of women's shoes in the United States.

When it came to building his latest yacht, Fisher had not taken a low-cost approach. The 225-foot vessel had a crew of twenty-two and eight different areas where as many as a dozen people could sit down for a meal. The interior spaces were inspired by the grand salons of the great transatlantic liners of the 1920s and 1930s.

Before they accepted the prize, Fisher and his wife, Anne, invited close to twenty people to join them on the stage. Then Anne, an architect who had planned the interior with the help of an Italian designer, went to the lectern, put on a pair of glasses, and began reading from typewritten remarks to describe the contributions of each member of the assemblage. By the time she got to the lawyer, the audience broke out in laughter. Looking up from her papers, Anne spoke sternly: "No no, the lawyer is very important—really." That was as specific as she got, but several people in the audience thought they understood the reference: in spite of what Von Allmen said about the unlikelihood that a shipyard would pay a penalty for a tardy delivery, the Fishers' lawyer apparently had extracted a substantial settlement from the shipyard that built *Lady Anne*.

Steve Rattner, the forty-six-year-old head of the merchant banking group at Donaldson, Lufkin & Jenrette, won the award for the best "refit" of a yacht. To better meet the needs of his young children, he had rebuilt a yacht that was originally launched in 2002. The "swimming platform" at the stern had been expanded, as had storage compartments for the "toys": Jet Skis, kayaks, and a pair of small sailboats.

Rattner was obviously thrilled with the result: the 168-foot-long *Helios 2*. "We love the lifestyle," he declared from the stage, "and we love the people you meet, everyone from the nineteen-year-old Australian deckhand to the billionaire. I can't imagine living without it."

The biggest winner of the evening was Tom Perkins, who was honored for his *Maltese Falcon,* the largest of the yachts being celebrated and the only one powered by sail. Inspired by nineteenth-century clipper ships, "the *Falcon,*" as Perkins called it, carried three carbon fiber masts, each of them close to twenty stories high. But its size was not the boat's most remarkable feature. In his professional life, Perkins had provided start-up capital to several companies that had transformed their industries—among them Genentech, Netscape, Google, and Amazon.com—and his yacht was also revolutionary. Unique among large sailing vessels, its enormous masts rotated to harness the wind more efficiently. That meant the masts were not supported by any kind of rigging. During the design phase, many had pronounced that impossible, and Perkins, a self-described "tech nerd," had played a central role in developing technologies that proved the skeptics wrong.

Perkins had taken an equally untraditional approach to the yacht's interior, insisting that it be sleekly modern and have an "open plan" and walls expansive enough to display large contemporary paintings. With glass panels that revealed the base of the masts and polished stone and metal floors, the vessel's interior looked less like a sailing yacht than something out of *Star Wars*.

ShowBoats is an industry publication, the cheerleading kind that inevitably focuses on the positives, but it was clear that Jill Bobrow, who had been editing yacht magazines for thirty years, was genuinely impressed. When Perkins made his way to the stage to pick up his fourth prize of the evening, she declared, "The *Maltese Falcon* is, quite simply, the most extraordinary yacht I have ever seen."

A few minutes later, a band that had been flown in from California began to play, and someone pressed a button to retract the ceiling. The group played an evocative blend of rock, jazz, and blues, and had a name that seemed completely out of sync with the rest of the festivities—"Big Dume"—but as the guests tilted back their heads to see the stars, it seemed, at least for the yacht owners and their facilitators, like the sky really was the only limit.

THE AWARDS made up just part of four days of celebration. One of the other highlights was a "yacht hop," a kind of progressive cocktail party during which owners and other guests wandered among the several hundred million dollars' worth of vessels docked along the eastern edge of Monte Carlo's main harbor. While not every owner joined the fun—*Lady Anne* was situated at one end of the pier, and a uniformed crew member was stationed at the head of its gangplank to make it clear that the Fishers had other plans—most did.

The crew at the yacht next to the *Lady Anne,* a 270-foot-long monster called *Floridian,* were particularly welcoming. Built by Greg Norman, the Australian pro golfer, the yacht was originally named *Aussie Rules,* and it carried a 42-foot sport-fishing boat called *No Rules,* along with a fleet of smaller recreational vessels and more than two hundred fishing rods. Norman had paid $70 million for the yacht and sold it for $90 million a few years later. Wayne Huizenga, the new owner, had founded three companies that became the dominant force of their industries—Waste Management, Blockbuster Video, and AutoNation. Huizenga renamed the yacht, painted the hull green, and replaced the platform that held the fishing boat with a landing pad for a twelve-seat helicopter. The helicopter was also green, and its tail carried the logo of the Miami Dolphins, which Huizenga co-owned. He was not on board for the party, but his son Wayne Jr. was a gracious host, pointing the way to the bar and a seafood buffet where the crab cakes were particularly popular.

The next yacht, *Alysia,* was even bigger. The 279-footer had eighteen guest cabins and a crew of thirty-six. Andreas Liveras, a

Cyprus-born shipping magnate, had built *Alysia,* as well as an almost identical sister ship, *Annaliesse,* with the idea that he would then be able to charter each of them for $900,000 a week, exclusive of fuel and food, or sell them to someone who did not want to wait to have a megayacht built from scratch. He hit the jackpot with *Annaliesse,* which he sold to the ruler of Dubai, Sheik Mohammed bin Rashid al-Maktoum. The sheik already owned the world's largest yacht, a 532-foot vessel that was originally commissioned by the younger brother of the sultan of Brunei, Prince Jefri Bolkiah. Sheik Mohammed had bought that vessel when it was still under construction in 2001, renamed it *Dubai,* and redesigned its interior so the top two of its seven decks would be reserved for his personal use. The other decks contained fifty guest suites and space for a crew of 115. *Dubai* was still being refurbished when the sheik bought *Annaliesse.* According to Billy Smith, Trinity's top salesman, who was participating in the yacht hop, "The sheik didn't want to wait, so Andreas earned a very substantial profit"—at least $30 million.

Farther down the dock sat *Ambrosia,* a 213-footer that belonged to Ambrose Young. The Hong Kong–based businessman stood out from the other owners, and not just because he was the only Asian among them. The contrast was particularly apparent when Von Allmen stepped on board wearing pale yellow pants and a lightweight checked jacket over a blue dress shirt—about the norm for most of the yacht hoppers. Ambrose was in all black, from his snug-fitting T-shirt to his stocking feet.

"Hi, I am your neighbor," Von Allmen said to Young, explaining that he owned *Linda Lou,* the next yacht down the dock.

Ambrosia's owner, preoccupied by a discussion with a member of his crew about the need for a lamb—a whole lamb—that he wanted to procure for a dinner he was planning, managed only a half-hearted handshake before turning away.

ONE DAY after the yacht hop, Jim and Nancy Baldwin were aboard their yacht, *Triton,* and sitting at a banquette that was adjacent and open to the galley. While most owners strove to create an upstairs-downstairs-like distance between themselves and their crew, the Baldwins had designed theirs to make it easier to chat with crew members, two of whom were then preparing a lobster salad.

Triton was a 163-foot "expedition yacht" outfitted with equipment for every imaginable type of adventure. Because Baldwin was an avid deep-sea fisherman, a crow's nest, the kind of open-air platform that was usually found on fishing boats, towered above the rest of the yacht. Reached by a small, unenclosed elevator, it could be used to spot fish, and it contained a helming station from which the yacht could be steered toward targets. On the main deck, a pair of fish-fighting chairs were mounted near the stern. If Baldwin hooked a big one, a 24-foot boat could be launched even as *Triton* was under way, allowing Baldwin to move from the mother ship to the more agile smaller craft without ever losing possession of his rod, a requirement under the rules of the International Game Fish Association.

Triton also carried a helicopter to facilitate onshore adventures. During a recent trip to Alaska, Baldwin told his guests to be on deck at seven o'clock one morning because they would be "going out for breakfast." Flying to a high-altitude meadow, the guests discovered that the crew had set up a table and chairs in a field of blooming spring flowers. After they enjoyed their bacon and eggs, the helicopter hauled the guests—and several kayaks—to the side of a fast-moving river. From there they paddled their way downstream to the bay, where *Triton* was anchored.

After lunch, Baldwin went to *Triton*'s main salon and switched on a television. He wanted to play the video that had been shot during a chopper trip to another Alaskan river. "We read about it in *National Geographic*—it's supposed to have more grizzlies than just about anywhere else," he explained. Once the video got going, it became apparent that some of the adventurers, including Nancy, who was operating the camera, had been on one side of the narrow river while others were standing on the opposite bank when five bears, including a mother trailed by her cub, loped down the middle of the river. "One false move, and it could have been all over," Baldwin said with a laugh. "I couldn't breathe."

Even *Triton*'s Mediterranean cruises contained elements of adventure. On the way to Monte Carlo, the helicopter had been in action almost every day, taking the Baldwins to mountains for high-altitude walks and to vineyards for tastings. But the Mediterranean was not the Baldwins' favorite cruising ground, and Monaco was far from their favorite port. They preferred places where theirs was the only yacht.

There were, Baldwin admitted, risks to his style of yachting. They had cruised through the Indonesian archipelago, where machine gun–wielding pirates were common. The Egyptian navy once fired shots across *Triton*'s bow because it had inadvertently entered a military zone. But Baldwin was undaunted. From Monaco he was making plans to head to Turkey, through the Suez Canal, down the Red Sea, and around the Arabian Peninsula to enter the Persian Gulf. Asked if it made sense to sail through a body of water that was close to a war zone and ridden with pirates, Baldwin waved his hand dismissively. "We don't have time to wait," he said. "There is no dress rehearsal for life."

LATER THAT AFTERNOON, Von Allmen was sitting in *Linda Lou*'s sky lounge. It was a stifling summer day but cool and absolutely silent on board. Looking across the harbor, he could see the promontory on which the royal palace was situated and the standard that was flying to indicate that Monaco's crown prince was in residence. He could also see *Ambrosia*. Obviously miffed by the short shrift he had been given by its owner, he claimed to be unimpressed by the yacht.

"They were obviously working to a tight budget," he said. "There are a lot of things that are just not right."

Opening his laptop computer, Von Allmen examined the latest drawings of *Lady Linda*'s exterior profile, which Evan Marshall had sent the day before. He was pleased to see his swooping windows but troubled by a decorative protrusion from the superstructure that started near the bow and ran toward the midsection of the boat, where it curved upward and disappeared. Sweeping his finger across the computer screen in a more extended arc to indicate what he believed would be a much better course for the curved protuberance, he said he was surprised that this was not obvious to Marshall. He was also frustrated because Marshall's drawings did not incorporate the large windows that Von Allmen had wanted for the master stateroom. "It looks to me like the top of the windows he's drawn would be at my eye level when I stand in the cabin. That's no good!"

4

Grinding It Out

Ocean: a body of water occupying about two-thirds of a
world made for man—who has no gills.

—*THE DEVIL'S DICTIONARY*, AMBROSE BIERCE

TWO MONTHS after the start of *Lady Linda*'s construction, in March
2008, Gale Tribble was working on the fuel tank module, so named
because it was a section of the hull that would eventually carry some
of the yacht's twenty-two thousand gallons of diesel. By then, several
other shipfitters and a number of welders were also working on the
project.

Shipfitters literally put vessels together, determining where
structural components belong and locking them into place with
short blasts of a welding torch. Welders are responsible for joining
the pieces more firmly together. Most fitters, Tribble among them,
believe their work is of a higher order; that mere welding is mindless
and boring. Many welders say they like the repetition, which they
describe as having the same kind of satisfaction as cutting grass.

For the most part, everyone worked independently. Tribble did
not need anyone to tell him how to identify the pieces he needed or
where they went. The plans contained all of the details. And once
he tacked things together, welders understood where they had to

do their work, because Tribble had used a black marker to indicate what needed to be joined. When there were conversations, they were short, in part because the yard was noisy: a constant screeching mix of sounds from the metal being cut, welded, and pounded, punctuated by moving equipment and alarms that sounded whenever one of the travel lifts was in motion. Like most workers, Tribble wore earplugs, something he had neglected to do when he was young, and probably the reason he was now hard of hearing.

Extreme heat has been used to join pieces of metal together since prehistoric times, but until the nineteenth century, it was generally done in forges by blacksmiths who pounded heated metals until they were merged. During the 1800s, portable technologies were developed, and they became economically efficient during World Wars I and II. Since then, the methodology has been basically unchanged.

No one has found a way to build large metal-hulled yachts that doesn't involve welding together thousands of pieces, one at a time.

The work has always been dangerous. The arc of electricity that Tribble's welding torch produced to create metal-melting heat also yielded a light so intense that it could damage the retina of an unprotected eye. Tribble believed those flashes of light were the reason he had needed cataract surgery a decade earlier. Even very brief exposures resulted in intense pain to unprotected eyes, followed by tears and an uncomfortable sensation that felt like they had been rubbed with sand. The protective glass of a welding helmet's mask provided full protection, but the mask also resulted in instant blindness: the glass lens was so dark that it was impossible to see anything once the helmet was lowered into place—until the trigger was pulled to activate the torch. This meant that Tribble had to turn it on before he could really see what he was doing.

The other challenge was that he sometimes had to hold the torch as well as the piece of metal he was seeking to attach, leaving him without a spare hand to lower his face mask. The best solution was to position the shield in such a way that it would fall into place with a shake or two of his head. There was a quicker but more dangerous alternative: a "blind tack," in which he lined up his torch, shut his eyes, and fired. Tribble admitted to taking this approach from time to time, but he knew it was unsafe, both because he could miss his intended target and because it would scorch the skin of his face, producing what looked and felt like a sunburn. Welding could also lead to burned hands and arms, particularly when the work was being done in tight or awkward positions. When even a small amount of molten metal hit the skin, it felt like being hit by a BB gun. Larger amounts felt like touching a hot stove. Tribble burned himself about once a week, and his forearms bore the evidence with a constellation of small white scars.

Supervisors stopped by *Lady Linda* only once or twice a day, but it was understood by everyone that they checked to see that structural elements were placed correctly and that it was possible to measure each laborer's productivity. Pieces that had been placed by Tribble and each of the other shipfitters could be counted because each of them marked his work with an employee number.

Even though shipfitters used tape measures, straightedges, and levels to check their work, errors were inevitable, and they were the source of tremendous frustration for Tribble, who rarely made mistakes himself. He took great pride in his work, and he believed that this, more than anything else, explained why he was good at what he did. "Some people are here just for the money," he said. "I am here for the money too—don't get me wrong—but I like what I do. If you don't have pride in what you're doing, things just aren't going to turn out right." When others made mistakes, Tribble was sometimes asked to do the remedial work. It was the only kind of work to which he objected: "I usually tell the supervisor, 'You should have the guy who messed it up fix it himself.'"

MOST OF the men—there were no women—working on *Lady Linda* did not share Gale Tribble's never-complain approach to things or the pride he had in his craft. "I'd rather have a desk job," said twenty-eight-year-old Thomas Nguyen. After his mother and father fled Vietnam in 1975, they settled in Oregon and had three children before they moved to New Orleans in 1995. Nguyen still lived with his parents, so he had to drive for more than an hour to and from work. "I don't have time for anything," he complained. "When I get home, it's late; I go to sleep." The only part of the day Nguyen enjoyed was listening to hip-hop music in his car—and even that was diminished by the knowledge that much of what he earned, $16.50 an hour, went to car loan payments. "What I need to do," he said, "is go to a community college somewhere and find a job that pays better."

Jay Lemoine had been a welder off and on for most of his working life. A thirty-eight-year-old native of Louisiana, he always wore a welding shirt, an obviously long-worn garment with leather patches covering the forearms and shoulders. Small brushes protruded from each of his breast pockets. They looked like toothbrushes, but the bristles were made of steel. He used them to clean surfaces before he welded them. The shirt was pockmarked with tiny black spots and holes, legacies of sparks that had flown from his welding torch. For most of the previous fifteen years, Lemoine had worked as an itinerant welder at various power plant construction projects and lived in an RV that he towed behind his car. He never lacked for work. During one eleven-month stretch, he logged ten hours or more a day, seven days a week. The money was great, but when he heard about friends who had started home-construction businesses after Katrina, Lemoine decided to go home and do the same. There too he found steady demand for his labor, but he was not prepared to handle the business side. After his biggest customer refused to pay bills amounting to $12,000, Lemoine gave up the business and returned to welding.

He liked working at Trinity more than at power plant sites, which were generally dirty and totally exposed to the outdoors, but he was not sure how long he would stay. "I don't want to do manual labor all my life," he said. He had recently heard that a beer and tobacco shop near where he was living might be up for sale, and he was thinking about trying to buy it. "I could sit on my butt all day, and it would never be too hot or cold."

Charles Lucas was more enthusiastic. An African-American who took great pride in his appearance, he wore a diamond in one ear and had a gold tooth that gleamed whenever he smiled, which was frequently. His most prominent feature was his moustache, which joined a carefully trimmed beard to form an almost perfect circle. Trinity generally sought to hire fully trained welders, but it had so many yachts to build that it was also creating new ones through on-the-job training. Lucas had started out as a general laborer, and at age forty-three, he was, thanks to Trinity, on his way to becoming a proficient welder.

"This is my field; I love it," Lucas declared from the interior of the fuel tank module. A weld holding together two components looks like caulk, or toothpaste, that had been squirted between the pieces. The edges of a good weld are smooth, and its thickness is consistent. Pointing to where he had used an indelible black marker to write his employee number—1035—next to one of his welds, Lucas traced his index finger over the mostly smooth joint. "My work wasn't looking anything like this a few months ago."

AT NINE O'CLOCK in the morning, after the horn signaled the start of a ten-minute break, Tribble retrieved a sticky bun and Coke from his cooler, and sat down on a toolbox. As soon as he finished eating, he lit a cigarette. Following this break, work continued until a thirty-minute lunch break at noon. After consuming his lunchtime sandwich, Tribble took a short walk outside, where he passed by various components that would be needed in the future: thousand-pound anchors, mechanical equipment and pumps, and a pair of large hot tubs that were lying on their sides.

The ten-hour workday did not end until four thirty. Because of its backlog of orders, Trinity had adopted the six-to-four-thirty schedule for Monday through Thursday. On Friday, the workday began at six and ended at two thirty. Having already worked forty hours, workers earned time-and-a-half pay for their Friday hours.

Trinity's forty-eight-hour workweek seemed unlikely to change anytime soon. While the pace of new contract signings with American customers had begun to slow, the company had a backlog of orders, and the weak dollar had bolstered demand from overseas. In fact, the last four contracts had been signed with foreigners, and salesman in chief Billy Smith was getting ready to travel to a boat show in Dubai. Smith, whose office was located just a couple of hundred feet from where *Lady Linda* was coming to life, said he was not worried by signs that the economy was losing some of its steam. His biggest worry was the soaring price of oil: not because it might cause customers to think twice about ordering a diesel-guzzling vessel—

fuel, in fact, represented a relatively small portion of the overall cost of operating a large yacht—but because it would cause the oil and gas industry to order more ships, making it more costly to retain welders and shipfitters.

FOR MOST of history, the owners of large pleasure vessels were members of royal families, so their access to the labor required to build and operate them was virtually unfettered. Several thousand years before Von Allmen starting building *Lady Linda,* Pharaoh Cheops, the Egyptian ruler best known for building the Great Pyramid at Giza, launched a shapely 140-foot-long craft. Ptolemy IV, Egypt's ruler two hundred years before the birth of Christ, built a vessel that was, even by modern standards, enormous. More than 400 feet long, it was powered by several hundred oarsmen.

One of Ptolemy's descendents, Cleopatra, commissioned a vessel that in 24 BC bore her across the Mediterranean Sea to meet Mark Antony, the ruler of the eastern portion of the Roman Empire. The luxuriously appointed vessel (depicted dramatically in the Oscar-winning 1963 film *Cleopatra,* featuring Elizabeth Taylor in the role of Egypt's queen) carried a pair of purple linen sails but was propelled by dozens of men who pulled at silver-tipped oars. Like modern-day yacht owners, Cleopatra hoped to make a memorable first impression—and evidently she succeeded. Virtually the entire population of the city of Tarsus gathered near the waterfront to see her waterborne palace glide toward land. Once the vessel was secured, Cleopatra declined Antony's invitation to go ashore. Instead, she asked him to visit her aboard the boat, which she considered to be an extension of Egyptian territory. When he arrived, Antony was directed to its largest room, the equivalent of today's main salon. With walls covered with purple-and-gold tapestries and copper mirrors, it was as ornate as a jewel box. Tables were laid with golden goblets and plates inlaid with jewels. Antony was said to have fallen immediately in love.

China's ancient rulers were also obsessed with the idea of large floating palaces. Chief among them was Yang Ti, a tyrannical emperor who is said to have come to power after he murdered his father and older brother in AD 604. His red-hulled yacht, called *The Little Red,* is believed to have incorporated grand reception halls and a throne room. Yang Ti forced millions of his subjects to build a series of interlocking canals that connected the fertile Yangtze River Basin to the population centers of the North. The canals' primary purpose was to move rice crops more efficiently, but they also facilitated the emperor's favored method of travel. *Little Red* was pulled by lines that were strapped to men who wore silk robes and young women who were said to be virgins.

It is not known when Europe's rulers first took to the sea, but a man believed to have been an Anglo-Saxon king from the seventh century was entombed next to a 90-foot vessel near the River Deben in the east of England. Filled with gold and silver jewelry along with armor and ceramics, the vessel, like most of the royal yachts that would be built during the next thousand years, was pushed by oars. One of the first sail-powered royal yachts was built by Queen Elizabeth I in 1588. The eighty-ton *Rat of Wight,* apparently so called because of its relative petiteness, was sailed by a crew of sixty. Since the *Rat,* every British monarch has had a yacht.

Charles Stuart, later Charles II, was particularly devoted to the sea. When Oliver Cromwell banished the monarchy in the mid-seventeenth century, Charles lived in Holland, then the Continent's most important trading center. With an unprecedented combination of wealth and seamanship, even nonroyal Dutchmen were building substantial vessels that had no purpose beyond pleasure. These boats offered a glimpse of what the future would bring: they were outfitted with kitchens and staffed by chefs who turned out elaborate meals. They were known as *jaght schips,* which meant "hunting ships," a name that had it origin in sixteenth-century vessels that were built to battle pirates. Charles II borrowed a vessel during his time in Holland. He enjoyed it so much that the Dutch government gave him a 52-foot craft replete with gilded cabins filled with paintings and sculptures. After Charles II returned to England as its king in 1660, he named the boat *Mary,* in honor of his sister. During the quarter century of his reign, he built at least twenty-five other luxuriously furnished boats. In England, the Dutch name for pleasure boats was altered slightly. They were called yachts.

THREE CENTURIES LATER, Trinity Yachts's relatively low-cost, nonunionized labor force was one of its most important competitive advantages—laborers in Europe were paid more than twice as much—which is why 2005's Hurricane Katrina had been such a serious threat. While none of the projects that had been under way in New Orleans was damaged badly by the hurricane, it was obvious that the facility would be unusable for several months. Without work, Trinity's employees would have dispersed.

John Dane understood the extent of the hurricane's devastation firsthand: not only was his waterfront home destroyed, but it had disappeared entirely from its foundation along with all of its contents. When he went to his New Orleans shipyard, it was literally underwater, and he knew that electricity or telephone service would not be restored anytime soon. Once he saw that the partially built yachts were okay, his greatest concern was retaining his employees. Some of his competitors were already spreading rumors suggesting that Trinity had been hit so badly that it was beyond recovery.

Working from his own yacht, which somehow had not been damaged, Dane purchased radio advertising to get out the word that Trinity would be back in business soon and that it would hand each worker $1,500 in cash assistance. Within a matter of days, he purchased an unused shipyard in Gulfport along with 104 mobile homes that would house employees who did not have anywhere else to live. Partially completed yachts were towed from New Orleans to the new facility, and just five weeks after the hurricane hit, there were more than seven hundred laborers working there, including eighty-three welders and sixty-five shipfitters.

AFTER A horn blast signaled the end of the workday, Gale Tribble punched his time card and headed toward the security gate where, every day, Trinity employees were required to open their lunch coolers to show a guard that they had not stolen tools or anything else. After he reached his truck and removed his coveralls, Tribble joined a lengthy procession of vehicles, almost all of them pickup trucks, making its way slowly toward Seaway Road.

Five miles into the ride home, he stopped at a corner store and purchased a thirty-two-ounce bottle of Miller Lite. Twenty minutes later, he pulled into his driveway and parked between his house and a mobile home where his daughter's family had lived before Katrina hit. Its walls were intact, but most of the roof had been torn away by the storm, and the interior was a total loss. Tribble's own house was largely unscathed.

The property surrounding Tribble's house was another story. It looked like the hurricane or perhaps a tornado had touched down and spun his belongings into a whirlwind of disarray, although Tribble admitted that he was largely to blame. A pile of asphalt shingles lay on one side of the house. Beyond that was a graveyard for several rusting washing machines and dryers along with a porcelain toilet and, not far from that, a plastic pool liner lying limply on the ground. A roofless shed contained a nonworking freezer and a cabinet with the power tools he used around the house. Next to the shed stood a pump for a well that had stopped working during the hurricane. The only organized part of the property was just outside the kitchen, where Tribble had used chicken wire to construct a car-sized enclosure into which he had thrown thousands of empty beer cans, the vast majority of which were Busch Lights.

Going inside, Tribble said hello to his thirty-three-year-old daughter, Melinda, and his two grandchildren, thirteen-year-old Damian and ten-year-old Shantell. Three chairs and a couch were jammed together, arm to arm, and lined up against the living-room wall opposite the television set, which was broadcasting a local news program. Four large sheets of gypsum board were sandwiched between the back of the couch and the wall. After Tribble's wife had died a few years earlier, his daughter and grandchildren moved in, and Tribble was planning to use the boards when he built an addition to the house. (Tribble's three other children, a second daughter and two sons, one a shipfitter and the other a welder, also lived in Pass Christian.)

Walking through the room, Tribble switched on an electric fireplace, which was against the wall that separated the living room from the kitchen. A photographic montage above the fireplace contained images of four of the yachts Trinity had completed in 2007. A Christmas gift from the company, it was still wrapped in the clear plastic in which it had come. Tribble pointed to the photographs with obvious pride. "I have worked on some really ugly-looking ships over the years," he said. "But look at these: they're sleek, they're beautiful. I don't build the whole boat—no one will ever see that little piece of it I was working on today—but I like the idea that I'm building boats that give people pleasure."

Sitting down in his favorite blue-and-green-striped chair, positioned directly across from the TV, Tribble opened a Busch Light. He stared at the newscaster, who was reporting on the war in Iraq, but he was not listening. Instead, he spoke about how he hoped to have a chance to go on *Lady Linda* when it was completed. "I would love to see what it's really like," he said, although his wistful tone suggested that he did not believe it would ever actually happen. He then admitted that he would be nervous about making such a visit. "I'd be afraid that I'd scratch something up."

Lighting up a cigarette, Tribble said nothing for a couple of minutes until he added, "I'm a poor person. I have a simple life. I can't have everything I want, but I have a comfortable life. And, you know, I don't really know if I'd like to be a multimillionaire. I'd probably have so many friends who wanted something from me that I would have to put up a ten-foot fence. I wouldn't like that part."

5

Flying Above the Clouds

IT WAS a warm summer day in July 2008, and Doug Von Allmen was aboard *Linda Lou,* his 197-foot Lürssen, as it lay at anchor near Saint-Tropez, France, after visits to Monaco and Cannes. Just after breakfast, he sat down with his laptop in the sky lounge to type out an email to Marshall: "Let's prepare a change order to add a garage to *Lady Linda.*"

Von Allmen was not suggesting the addition of a garage for a car. He was thinking about a concealed compartment for the two smaller boats, or tenders, that *Lady Linda* would carry to shuttle the Von Allmens and their guests to and from the mother ship. A garage would eliminate the need to store them on the top deck, where they would block views and detract from its appearance. The cost would be substantial—at least $3 million, Von Allmen guessed—but he worried that the price of *not* having a garage would be even greater in terms of how the yacht would be judged and valued.

Tender garages were first introduced in the 1980s. Since then, while most American owners had been willing to live with on-deck storage, Europeans had come to regard that as distasteful—something like parking a car in the front yard of a house. Von Allmen had recently come to embrace the European sensibility. Almost all of the newest generation of large yachts featured garages. Von Allmen was also guided by an overarching principle of the big-boat marketplace: the most highly regarded yachts created the impression that no expense had been spared. Any indication that a yacht's designer had been constrained by a budget was a major black mark.

The collapse of a Wall Street firm, Bear Stearns, four months before he sent his email had foreshadowed an economic storm that was by then gathering force. But Von Allmen was not overly concerned. He believed that he—and most owners of the very largest yachts—were still flying above the darkening clouds. Prospective yacht owners continued to pay multimillion-dollar payments to contract holders willing to give up their place in the production queue, and newly completed yachts were still selling for much more than the cost of building them. A few months earlier, a wealthy Russian had offered to buy *Linda Lou* for $100 million, double what Von Allmen had paid for it. He rejected the offer.

Perhaps Von Allmen should have recognized the frothy exuberance as a symptom of what was to come, but he had persuaded himself that it was simply a matter of supply and demand.

LINDA LOU had been Von Allmen's greatest extravagance. After having acquired more than fifty companies during the second phase of his career as a private equity investor, his net worth had become very substantial. One of his businesses, a Tulsa, Oklahoma–based firm that supplied beauty products to more than three thousand hair salons across Oklahoma, Arkansas, Kansas, and Missouri, was particularly successful. The company, Beauty Alliance, was large enough to negotiate advantageous prices from manufacturers—and, thanks to its close relationships with salon owners, able to maintain an almost ironclad grip over its customers. Von Allmen became so bullish about its potential that he traded ownership shares in other companies with his partners, the Olsons, to become its sole owner.

As an adult, Von Allmen's health had been good, but his father had died young. So in 2003 he had decided that it was time to *really* start enjoying his wealth by building a very big yacht. Unlike his previous vessels, which had all been American made, Von Allmen decided that *Linda Lou* would come from Europe. He had come to understand that the very best yachts were made by one of two firms: Feadship, the Dutch company that built Malcolm Forbes's *High-lander,* or Lürssen, which was then building Larry Ellison's *Rising Sun.* Von Allmen thought of the differences in terms of cars: Trinity and some of the other American builders made excellent products, but it was the equivalent of a Mercedes or a BMW. Lürssen, which he regarded as the best of the best, was turning out Bentleys.

Linda Lou, with its $50 million price tag, would cost more than all of his previous boats combined, or, for that matter, far more than any of the companies he had bought during his business career. "It was slightly crazy," he said a few years later. "But Lürssens are the finest boats in the world, and I just had to have one." Von Allmen agreed to build the vessel even though he recognized that it would not be well suited to his needs. A "full displacement" boat, it would have a draft of eleven feet six inches: too deep to dock behind his Fort Lauderdale house or to enter many of his favorite harbors in Florida and the Bahamas. Because of those limitations, he decided to commission the building of an additional yacht, a 157-foot Trinity.

Even in the context of a supercharged economy, the simultaneous construction of *two* enormous yachts was virtually unprecedented, but Von Allmen had persuaded himself that it made sense. *Linda Lou* would spend most of its time in the Mediterranean and perhaps take longer voyages to the South Pacific. The "little boat," which would cost $22 million, would spend most of its time closer to home. What Von Allmen did not foresee was that both boats would be delivered

at almost exactly the same time. The Trinity was supposed to be
completed in 2005, but it was delayed by Katrina. As a result, he
took delivery of both yachts in September 2006, one month after his
sixty-fifth birthday. The feat was celebrated in a cover story in *Show-
Boats* entitled "Two to Tango: It Takes a Lürssen AND a Trinity to
Cover the Dance Floor for This Cruising Couple."

At the time, Von Allmen was not worried about the enormous
financial burdens the two vessels would entail, each of them with
full-time crews and never-ending maintenance requirements. He
knew that an age-old rule of thumb about boat ownership—the
annual cost of maintaining and operating a boat is equal to at least
10 percent of its purchase price—held true regardless of its size. Von
Allmen was focused on the positives: the new yachts were worth far
more than he had paid for them, and his net worth had never been
greater. Beauty Alliance was supplying 125,000 salons throughout
the South and Midwest, with annual sales of $372 million. Three
months before Von Allmen took delivery of his two big boats, he
had agreed to sell 30 percent of the company to L'Oréal, the French
cosmetics giant. A few months after their delivery, L'Oréal paid Von
Allmen $260 million for the rest of the company.

Von Allmen also felt emboldened by the explosive growth of
American wealth. According to *Forbes*, the United States had just
thirteen billionaires in 1982. Back then, anyone worth more than
$75 million was given a place on the magazine's inaugural list of the
four hundred wealthiest Americans. By early 2006, the country had
several hundred billionaires, and everyone on the magazine's "rich list"
was worth more than $1 billion. There were two main drivers in the
explosion of wealth: the economy had grown, and the portion of the
benefits going to the very wealthy had soared. In 1982 the Americans
with the largest incomes—the top 1 percent—took home 10 percent
of the nation's overall income. In 2007 the top 1 percent took more
than twice that: almost 23 percent, close to the all-time high of 24
percent that had been set during the Roaring Twenties, in 1928.

With such extraordinary wealth accumulation, Von Allmen believed the demand for yachts would continue to outstrip the capacity of the yacht-building industry. Therefore, he also believed he could convert either one of his big boats into cash whenever he chose.

Von Allmen was so confident that in late 2006 he had decided to build yet another yacht: the 187-footer that would become *Lady Linda*. It would be substantially larger than the 157-foot Trinity, and he hoped it would have the same quality as the Lürssen. It would also have another very important attribute: unlike the Lürssen, it could be docked behind his house. At some point, Von Allmen planned to sell one or possibly both of his already complete yachts. *Lady Linda* would be the keeper.

ONE OF the yachts that had changed Von Allmen's thinking about the importance of having a garage had recently visited Saint-Tropez, where it had become the talk of the town. Longer than a football field, it carried a one-letter name:—*A*. Even by sky-is-the-limit superyacht standards, it is a jaw-dropper: 390 feet long, it cost more than $300 million to build, has 23,000 square feet of living space, and burns through 690 gallons of diesel an hour. But what truly sets *A* apart is its shape: its bow slopes away from the boat in the way of a snowplow or a World War I battleship.

A's garage is a vast compartment that opens out to both sides of the hull. The space is large enough to house two 30-foot tenders, which can be launched by a pair of telescoping cranes. When both tenders are removed, the space was designed to become something else: a discotheque. A disco with a difference: the ceiling, made of glass, also serves as the floor of a large swimming pool, making it possible for those on the dance floor to watch swimmers overhead.

Andrey Melnichenko, *A*'s thirty-six-year-old owner, is a Russian oligarch, one of the band of relatively young men who had ridden a tidal wave of petroleum wealth during Vladimir Putin's leadership to amass astonishing fortunes almost overnight. The oligarchs had become a dominant force in the market for the very biggest yachts, a replay of what happened in the 1970s, when the soaring price of oil put a much larger share of the world's wealth in Arab hands. Arabs still owned the world's four largest yachts. After Sheik Mohammed's *Dubai,* the next largest was *Abdulaziz,* a 482-footer owned by the Saudi royal family. *El Horriya,* Egypt's 478-foot presidential yacht, ranked third. Another Saudi-owned yacht, the 459-foot *Al Salamah,* was fourth. But the Russian oligarchs were well on their way to shaking up the rankings. Young and impetuous, they were motivated not just by ego but also by concerns about their security. A large yacht could serve as a comfortable safe haven; if filled with valuable works of art, it could also function as a portable storehouse of wealth.

Roman Abramovich, the forty-one-year-old owner of Britain's Chelsea football club, was the runaway leader of the oligarch-yachtsmen. He owned three monster yachts, the biggest of which, the 377-foot-long *Pelorus,* was originally built for a Saudi prince. *A* was 13 feet longer than *Pelorus,* but Abramovich had already taken steps to reclaim his title by commissioning a *much* larger yacht, one that would carry a submarine and be protected by, among other things, a sophisticated missile-detection system. At 557 feet, it would have a crew of more than fifty and displace *Dubai* as the world's largest yacht. Fittingly, it would be called *Eclipse.*

Von Allmen regarded the Russian yachtsmen as a mixed blessing. While he was happy that they were energizing the market, the ways in which they threw around their money were not without downsides. During most of his previous Mediterranean cruises, Von Allmen had rented dock space at various ports. His yacht would be positioned in such a way that its stern would overlook the main promenade. "That way we could spend our afternoons watching the people who were watching us," Von Allmen explained with a chuckle. But now, thanks to the Russians, the economics involved in securing dock space had changed. The nominal cost was relatively low, but the harbor masters in some ports, many of them political appointees, expected to be compensated with tips. Until recently, the standard amount for a large yacht had been a few thousand dollars per day, but with the Russian influx the expectations had inflated to the point that Von Allmen had begun to spend most nights at anchor. "The Russians," he complained, "spend money like there's no tomorrow."

In London, Von Allmen's request for a garage came as a shock to Marshall. He understood the benefits of a garage as well as anyone. He was in the midst of designing a garage-equipped yacht that was just 112 feet long. But adding one to *Lady Linda* at this stage would require an enormous amount of reengineering. As he sat at his desk attempting to find a way to wedge a new compartment into a vessel that was already under construction, he came to the conclusion that its overall length would probably have to be extended by several feet.

But his bigger concern was height constraints. The top of *Lady Linda*'s superstructure was, by the standards of a boat its size, close to the water. Marshall had wanted it that way because it would result in a sleek and elegant profile, but it left very little vertical space for a garage. The only solution he could come up with would require raising the rear portion of the main deck's floor by about a foot— and that would mean adding a step between the main salon and the outdoor deck directly behind it. Someone leaving the salon would have to step up to reach the outdoor deck at the stern. Marshall believed that would be a terrible mistake. Inevitably, people would trip, sending drinks and platters of food flying. Worse still, it would look like he, the designer, had made a mistake or that a compromise had been accepted. And even with the step, the garage height would be just seven feet, too low to accommodate the most desirable types of tenders.

Marshall was already planning to meet Von Allmen in Saint-Tropez a couple of days later to review his latest thoughts about *Lady Linda*'s interior design. As he prepared for the meeting, he realized that discussion would probably end up being displaced by one about the garage. Having assumed that the major decisions about the yacht's shape and dimensions had already been settled, he was annoyed, but Marshall was in a business in which the client was unquestionably always right, so he created several conceptual plans on his computer to show how a garage might be accommodated. After he printed them, he marked the required step with a thick black line to ensure that Von Allmen fully understood the garage's design-marring impact.

AT FOUR THIRTY in the morning, Marshall was standing at the front door of his house, waiting for a taxi that would get him to London's Heathrow Airport for a seven o'clock flight to Nice, France. Once he landed, he rented a car and began driving west. Everything was fine until he merged into the winding coastal road that led to tourist-choked Saint-Tropez. With the harbor and *Linda Lou* in sight, traffic had come to a virtual halt. After spending close to an hour crawling along at something less than walking speed, he pulled into a parking lot a half mile from the center of town and dialed Von Allmen's cell phone to ask if one of *Linda Lou*'s tenders could be sent to a nearby dock. Marshall had hoped to begin his meeting by one o'clock, but by the time he boarded *Linda Lou* and a steward directed him to a mahogany table that was outside but sheltered from the sun, it was already two thirty. Since he needed to leave by four o'clock in order to catch a seven thirty flight back to London, the last one of the day, he was already worried about the time, so he quickly unrolled the drawing that showed what *Lady Linda*'s profile would look like with a garage and five extra feet of length.

One of the secrets of yacht design is that adding length almost always benefits a vessel's appearance. Most modern-day yachts have far larger superstructures and more interior space than similarly sized boats did in the past, which is why many of them look so bulbous and top heavy. Lengthening a hull without enlarging the superstructure generally leads to a shape that more closely resembles that of a classic boat. But the situation with *Lady Linda* was different. Because construction had begun, it would not be a matter of stretching the overall profile; it would be more like tacking five feet of length onto the rear end. However, while Marshall did not like the result, Von Allmen did not seem to have a problem with it. Focusing on the dimension itself, he asked, "So, what does this do to the length?"

"It would get us to one hundred ninety-three feet; about fifty-nine meters."

"Why don't we add a bit more to make it spot-on sixty meters?"

Although Marshall did not think it would actually come to that, he quickly agreed. "Why not?" he said. "I like round numbers, and it's just a couple of feet more."

But then, before Von Allmen became any more excited, Marshall burst the bubble: "The big problem with this is that we would need to add a step on the main deck." Pointing to the bold black line, he added, "You would have to step up from the main salon to the deck outside, which is obviously not ideal."

"No, no, no!" Von Allmen said. "We can't have a step there."

After studying the plan a bit longer, Von Allmen added, "If we absolutely have to have a step, we need to put it somewhere else." Pointing toward the center of the main salon, he suggested that it could be placed there to create a "split-level" room in which the bar area near the stern would be higher than the rest of the room. He suggested that using different floor levels to divide the room into two different sections might even be a positive. Marshall disagreed. He thought the resulting ceiling height in the bar area would feel much too low and that a step would look like an error. However, since this was not a possibility he had explored, he said he would go back to the drawing board and discuss the options with the engineers at Trinity.

When the garage discussion was over, Linda joined the meeting to talk about *Lady Linda*'s interior design. They were planning to have an in-depth discussion about the interior in New York in October, but Marshall hoped to lay the groundwork for that meeting by floating a few ideas. But he did not have much time. He flipped through only a few drawings before boarding the tender that returned him to his car at four thirty.

Once again, he was mired in traffic. In search of a better route, Marshall turned onto a side road and became hopelessly lost. It was soon obvious that his flight would leave without him. Then the battery of his cell phone expired. As he wondered whether he would be able to find a hotel in the height of the summer holiday season, he could not help but think how different things would be back aboard *Linda Lou*. By now, the crew had probably uncorked a spectacular bottle of wine, and the Von Allmens were no doubt lounging on the aft deck watching the other boats move about Saint-Tropez's harbor.

6

Gilded Barges

WHEN MARSHALL arrived at the Von Allmens' Manhattan apartment on October 7, 2008, to make the more detailed presentation of his ideas for *Lady Linda*'s interior design, the financial meltdown was already under way and Von Allmen had become concerned. He had recently taken a close look at his personal expenses to discover that the operating costs of his two existing yachts represented 85 percent of his total expenditures. The cost of building and maintaining *Lady Linda* would add substantially to the burden. "I'm probably going to end up owning three very large boats," he said before the meeting began. "We'll have to see if I can afford them."

The apartment was another great extravagance. A duplex on the seventy-fourth and seventy-fifth floors of the Time Warner Center, its glass walls revealed an extraordinary panorama. From Central Park and the crush of office towers in Midtown, it stretched out to the George Washington Bridge and the western approaches to Long Island Sound. The view was so spectacular that it did not quite register as real. The quiet added to that impression. Although the meeting began at eight thirty, the height of New York's morning rush hour, the street noise was inaudible.

It would be a day of extraordinary financial chaos. The Dow Jones Industrial Average would continue its freefall by losing more than 500 points. The new reality had arrived all too suddenly. One month before the meeting, Lehman Brothers, the 158-year-old financial firm, had failed, and Merrill Lynch admitted to having lost more than $50 billion from bonds created out of residential mortgages. Unthinkable things had been happening ever since. And while the value of Von Allmen's financial assets was plummeting, most of his expenses were fixed—the consequence being that his lifestyle was rapidly becoming unsustainable.

With so much uncertainty, he was now thinking about trying to sell *both* of his current yachts. He had no idea what they were worth, although he knew no one was going to pay anything close to $100 million for *Linda Lou* anymore. Until recently, he believed his smaller yacht, the 157-footer, which had cost $22 million to build, was worth at least $30 million. But now he guessed its value had declined as dramatically as stock prices, probably more so. In truth, values were impossible to determine because there were virtually no buyers.

As Von Allmen searched for ways to curtail his lifestyle expenses, *Lady Linda*'s garage was one of the first casualties. In fact, his whole approach to the new boat was in flux. Though he had not said anything to Marshall about abandoning his commitment to creating a groundbreaking showpiece, financial constraints had become a factor in his decision making.

THE DESIGN and ownership of yachts have always followed the rise and fall of larger economic tides. America's first large-scale pleasure yacht was a 100-foot square rigger launched in 1816 by George Crowninshield Jr., the son of a Boston-based ship owner and privateer. Pioneering what would become a tradition for American yacht owners all the way up to the Von Allmens, Crowninshield's vessel—which he named *Cleopatra's Barge*—sailed across the Atlantic

Ocean shortly after it was completed to undertake an extensive tour of Mediterranean ports.

After a steam-powered ship crossed the Atlantic in 1838, yacht owners were quick to recognize the possibilities, although there was also reluctance. At the Royal Yacht Squadron, England's most prestigious yacht club, steam propulsion was deemed to be incompatible with the club's goal of promoting seamanship, and a resolution was distributed to the membership: "No vessel propelled by steam shall be admitted into the club, and any member applying a steam-engine to his yacht shall be disqualified thereby and cease to be a member."

The edict would not stand for long. One of the early steam advocates was Queen Victoria, the squadron's only female member. She had become so frustrated during a breeze-challenged voyage to Scotland that the royal sailboat was ultimately towed by a pair of steam-powered paddle wheelers. In 1843 she built her own paddle wheeler, the 225-foot *Victoria and Albert*. One year later, the squadron permitted members to utilize engines—as long as they were substantial, at least 100 horsepower. Victoria went on to build a 300-foot steam yacht, the *Victoria and Albert II*. Like the earlier version, it was a paddle wheeler, even though propellers had become the more popular propulsion option.

In America, Cornelius Vanderbilt led the way into the steam-yacht era. Starting with a single ferry that shuttled cargo and passengers to points around New York Harbor, "Commodore" Vanderbilt assembled an empire of steamship lines and railroads that made him America's wealthiest person. In 1853 he launched the country's first steam yacht, the 270-foot *North Star*, which consumed fourteen tons of coal a day to turn a pair of 34-foot-diameter paddle wheels. Like Crowninshield, Vanderbilt undertook a grand tour of Europe, joined by ten of his twelve children. They lounged their way across the Atlantic in sumptuous cabins that had been furnished with Louis XV furniture, velvet cushions, and silk curtains. Meals were served in a marble-walled dining room beneath a ceiling adorned with medallion portraits of George Washington, Ben Franklin, and other famous Americans. During a three-month voyage, *North Star* paid visits to England as well as ports in the Mediterranean and Baltic Seas.

For Vanderbilt, who was then fifty-nine, this was not just a pleasure cruise. He also wanted to present the Old World with an arresting symbol of America's triumphant economic success. Shortly after *North Star* arrived in England, London's *Daily News* published an editorial that made the connections between the "monster steamer," its owner's fortune, and the country that had made both possible: "America was not known four centuries ago; yet she turns out her Vanderbilts, small and large, every year. America . . . is the great arena in which the individual energies of man, uncramped by oppressive social institutions or absurd social traditions, have full play, and arrive at gigantic development."

But Vanderbilt was ill suited to yachting life. The difficulty of communicating with his office was a particular frustration, especially after he learned that two of his partners established a steamship line that was harmful to his business interests during his absence. Not long after he returned to New York, Vanderbilt sent them a letter that was also published in several major newspapers: "Gentlemen, You have undertaken to cheat me. I won't sue you, for the law is too slow. I will ruin you. Yours truly, Cornelius Vanderbilt." Over time he did just that. And he gave up his yacht, turning it into a passenger liner that could accommodate hundreds of fare-paying customers.

Vanderbilt's fortune was ultimately worth more than $100 million—more, in present-day terms, than that of Bill Gates or Warren Buffett—and it enabled several of his descendents to become very enthusiastic yachtsmen. William K. Vanderbilt, one of the Commodore's grandsons, built a 285-foot steamship, the nation's largest. After it crashed into a commercial vessel near Nantucket Island, off the coast of Massachusetts, and sank in 1892, William ordered an even larger replacement. A great-grandson, Harold S. Vanderbilt, won three America's Cup competitions. Another great-grandson,

Cornelius III, also won the Cup, and he bought a steam yacht that he renamed *North Star.* Although it was not as large as the original, it was judged to be more luxurious.

The Vanderbilts were joined by self-made men who had capitalized on the availability of electricity and engines to create an array of new industries. At a time when taxes and restraints on monopolistic behavior were almost nonexistent, tremendous fortunes were amassed with astonishing speed. Grand houses were erected in and around Manhattan and along the coasts of Rhode Island, Maine, and Florida—and yachts became the favored method for moving among them and to Europe.

They also became something more: the hallmark for a new and very American kind of nobility. And as Vanderbilt had hoped, yachts were seen not as symbols of inequality but of achievement. Newspapers reported on even routine voyages. "Col. Astor's Steam Yacht Had an Uneventful Voyage from Venice" was the *New York Times* headline for an 1899 account of the latest movements of a yacht belonging to John Jacob Astor IV, who would die aboard the *Titanic* thirteen years later. "She passed Gibraltar on May 1, and steamed to Bermuda, making 3,000 miles without stopping, and reaching Bermuda May 15, remaining there two days for coal," the article reported. "A three-quarter rate of speed was maintained through the entire voyage, which was uneventful."

J.P. Morgan, a linchpin for many of the Gilded Age's fortunes, also became its leading yachtsman. Ever since he first crossed the Atlantic aboard a square rigger as a sickly fifteen-year-old, he was convinced that his health benefited from time on the water. Over a thirty-year period, he owned three large vessels, all of them having glossy black hulls, narrow clipper ship–like bows, and carrying the name *Corsair.* He bought the first, a 185-foot steamer, in 1882 to take him between Manhattan and his weekend home up the Hudson River near West Point, New York. With silk upholstering and working fireplaces, it was an elegant ride. After Morgan joined America's most prestigious association of yacht owners, the New York Yacht Club, he donated the land on which its Manhattan clubhouse was built, and he commissioned the second *Corsair,* a 238-footer, in 1890. Unfortunately for Morgan, it was requisitioned by the US Navy for use in the Spanish-American War, just after he was elected the club's commodore, so he ordered up a third *Corsair.* It was similar to its predecessors, but, at 304 feet, much larger, and it was designed to carry a substantial number of guests. The linen closets contained 84 linen tablecloths, 177 pillow cases, and 670 towels.

Given the scale of his yachts, it is not surprising that Morgan is credited with what remains the famous line about the cost of yacht ownership, words that are undiminished by the probability that they are apocryphal. According to legend, a wealthy oilman partner of John D. Rockefeller's, Henry Clay Pierce, asked, "How much does it cost to run a yacht?" Morgan was said to have declared, "You have no right to own a yacht if you ask that question."

© Beken of Cowes

J.P. Morgan's *Corsair II.*

The purpose of the *Corsairs* went beyond pleasure. In 1885 Morgan invited the presidents of two major railroads, the New York Central Railroad Company and the Pennsylvania Railroad, to come aboard on a steamy July morning to discuss disputes that endangered the profits of the New York company, in which he had a substantial holding. Once the yacht left its dock, Morgan announced that no one would disembark until everyone agreed to put an end to their "ruinous" competition.

A few years later, an American president, Grover Cleveland, utilized the distance that could be put between a yacht and the rest of the world for a different purpose. At a time when the country's economy was in crisis, his doctors had found a cancerous growth on his jaw. Not wanting worries about his health to contribute to a financial panic, the president boarded a friend's 138-foot steamer in Manhattan for what was said to be a vacation. In fact, the yacht had been equipped with an operating room, and surgery was conducted as it made its way eastward through Long Island Sound. When the president disembarked five days later, he had recuperated to the point that he could get away with complaining about what he called a terrible toothache. By the time the cruise's actual nature was revealed, his recovery was complete.

The era's most colorful big-boat owner was newspaper publisher James Gordon Bennett Jr. Having inherited the profit-gushing *New York Herald* from his father, in 1882 he took delivery of *Namouna,* a 227-foot steamer that had a fifty-person crew and incorporated a design innovation that would become standard: on sailing yachts, the master stateroom had always been located near the stern, the most stable part of the boat. But given the soot produced by coal-fired boilers, Bennett decided to place his stateroom close to the bow. Like most of the princes of the Gilded Age, he never let costs get in the way of his recreation. At a time when most American families lived on less than $500 a year, *Namouna*'s annual operating costs amounted to $150,000. His next yacht, a 314-footer that was completed in 1900, cost $600,000 to build and carried a hundred-person crew as well as an Alderney cow to provide passengers with fresh milk. Bennett's lifestyle, which also involved large homes and private railroad cars, eventually overwhelmed his resources. "Yachting had been a means of self-gratification as epic in scale as the energies of the land that produced him," wrote yachting historian John Rousmaniere. "When he died in 1918, at the age of 77, he was nearly broke, having squandered an estimated $40 million."

Following World War I, yacht building resumed on the back of a postwar economic boom. Indeed, some of the very largest yachts in all of history were assembled during the years between the Great War and the Great Depression: the Roaring Twenties.

Another leap in technology—the diesel engine—had helped to spur things. Diesels had two important advantages: they emitted less soot and smoke than coal-burning boilers, and because they could generate more power from a given volume of fuel, they required less space. The imposition of Prohibition in 1920 gave yachts additional purpose. Liquor could be consumed legally three miles from the American coastline, and the privacy of a yacht facilitated imbibing even closer to shore.

By then, some owners had found uses for their yachts that went beyond seasonal migrations up and down the East Coast and to Europe. William K. Vanderbilt Jr., one of the Commodore's great-grandsons, took his 212-foot *Ara* and 264-foot *Alva* on seven expeditions, two of them global circumnavigations that were similar to the kinds of adventures Jim and Nancy Baldwin would undertake almost a century later. *Alva* carried a seaplane as well as commercial fishing nets that were used both to catch exotic types of fish and to protect swimming passengers from sharks. During visits to the Galápagos Islands, the China Sea, and Australia's Great Barrier Reef, Vanderbilt and his crew collected hundreds of marine animals, including dozens of previously unknown species.

The most voracious yacht owner of the time was a woman. Emily

Roebling Cadwalader, the granddaughter of the man who built the Brooklyn Bridge, commissioned three yachts in quick succession, each of them more than one hundred feet larger than its predecessor. The first, a 185-footer, was completed in 1926; the second, a 294-footer, was launched two years later. The third, an astonishing 408 feet in length, cost $4 million to build and was the largest privately owned yacht the world had ever seen. It was so big that it could not enter many harbors and could not be accommodated by many docks. Cadwalader also had another, more pressing problem: when the yacht was launched in 1931, the American economy was spiraling downward into the Great Depression. When she put it up for sale a few years later, there were no buyers until the Turkish government bought it for about a fourth of what it had cost to build.

The Depression did not put an end to every yachting life. E. F. Hutton, the brokerage founder, and his wife, Marjorie Merriweather Post, an heir to the cereal fortune, replaced their 203-foot schooner with a 316-foot diesel-powered yacht that was completed in 1931. Mrs. Hutton, the sole owner after the couple divorced, continued to use the yacht and employ its seventy-two-person crew. She said it was her contribution to maintaining economic activity.

But as the crisis deepened, most of the other giants were retired. Costs were not the only factor. With the tough times, the distribution of the nation's wealth was becoming a political issue even as much of it was vanishing. Conspicuous consumption—a term that had been coined in 1899 by economist Thorstein Veblen—had suddenly gone out of fashion.

COST CUTTING was not what Marshall was thinking about when he prepared for the design meeting. It wasn't that he was unaware of the economic turmoil. Indeed, all of the conversations he had been having with prospective clients about possible new projects had suddenly ceased, and he worried that some of his current projects could be abandoned. But with *Lady Linda,* he saw no alternative but to press on in accordance with the Von Allmens' original aspirations. And given that this would be the project's first full-blown design meeting, he guessed it would turn out to be the most important in determining what the interior spaces would look like.

As the meeting began, Von Allmen was seated at a round table in the living room, with his back to the windows. Marshall, sitting to Von Allmen's right, held up a rendering of the vessel's main entryway and the adjacent staircase. The staircase walls were shown as being covered by a striking image he had borrowed from the *Normandie,* the French ship that was thought to be the world's most opulent ocean liner when it was launched in 1935: a mural depicting a mythical scene of horses and godlike humans orbiting a golden sun. During an era when passenger ships were objects of national pride, the *Normandie* had been loaded with artworks to demonstrate France's cultural superiority. For the rendering, Marshall had reproduced a photograph of *The Chariot of Aurora,* the gilded relief that adorned the ship's grand salon.

Marshall's initial thought was to incorporate the image just to introduce the concept of using a work of art to sheath the stairwell, but as he sat in the apartment, he began to think a version of this specific artwork might appeal to them. The long wall opposite the living room windows was dominated by a large painting of an industrial scene by Maria Simpson, who had trained with Diego Rivera, the famous muralist. First shown at the 1939 Golden Gate Exposition, it was created at around the same time as the *Normandie.* Because Simpson's work obviously appealed to the Von Allmens, Marshall thought there was a good chance they would also like *The Chariot of Aurora.*

Speaking quickly but with emphasis, hoping his enthusiasm and the art would combine to produce an irresistible force, Marshall began, "This would make a *very* strong impression. You'd step on board, and *bang*—you would know you were entering a very special yacht!"

Pivoting her head almost imperceptibly from side to side, Linda Von Allmen spent a few seconds trying to imagine what the mural would look like in real life before she pronounced, "It's great—I really like it!"

As always, Von Allmen was more difficult to read. He tended to focus on the details, sometimes obsessively, and his initial reactions were often dominated by things he did not like. Right now, he was thinking about the stairs shown in the rendering and the need to prevent them from creaking. Some of the steps on his current Trinity had always made noise.

"Trinity just doesn't know how to make a good set of stairs," he said. "We have to make sure that they get this one right."

A successful design presentation requires an element of theater, together with a feeling of momentum that can develop only if there is a favorable first impression. No client likes everything, but success depends on maintaining a sense, from the very beginning and all the way to the end, that the pluses are outweighing the minuses. If there are too many negatives—even if they are related to issues of minor importance—momentum is lost, and nothing looks right.

Rather than risk getting bogged down in a discussion about stairs, Marshall moved on to a rendering of the master bedroom. The focal point was the bed itself and its headboard, which contained a panel of intricately etched glass. Gesturing toward the etched glass, Marshall said, "It could have impressions of fish or birds; maybe a peacock. The idea is to backlight the glass to make it luminescent. It could be spectacular." Von Allmen was skeptical about the glass. In fact, although he didn't say so, Marshall had concerns of his own. If it was done right—which required a tasteful design, the absence of colored glass, and skilled craftsmanship—he thought it would be an elegant means of providing the "wow" factor he believed every room should have. Done poorly, it would be a gaudy embarrassment.

The next rendering was of the wall opposite the bed, which showed a large painting centered above a five-foot-long cabinet. The middle section of the cabinet was bowed, a reflection of Marshall's effort to carry the curves of the yacht's exterior profile to the inside. The painting, and what looked like a single canvas, would actually consist of two panels that concealed a forty-two-inch television screen; with the push of a button, the panels would slide apart. The painting was shown as square because Marshall thought that would be more effective than a horizontal artwork in masking what was behind the panels.

"I have used glass as a feature, and I've tried to put some pizzazz into everything," Marshall said of the compartment's overall appearance. "There are curves throughout, which give a romantic feel to the furniture—elegant but sensuous, too."

The last rendering showed the main salon, which would share the main deck with the master stateroom and would be the yacht's largest and grandest space. In his previous yachts, the compartment was also a great frustration to Von Allmen because he knew it would rarely be used. It was something like the formal living room of a house that was used only on holidays. Marshall had divided the space into three areas that would have different functions but would not be separated by partitions: a bar near the stern, a dining area toward the bow, and in between, a spacious section for seating. Unlike the other compartments, Marshall had not sought to give the main salon a single visual focal point. Fifty feet long, it was too big for that, he thought. "If we get this right, it will be a feast of details, like a beautiful symphony that keeps on building," he suggested. "If there are no bum notes, it will be stunning."

The final part of Marshall's presentation was the sky lounge. He did not have a rendering. Instead, he had come with nine conceptual drawings sketched out by hand, each showing a somewhat different approach. The only consistency among them was an unbroken stretch of cabinetry running along both sides of the room beneath the large windows. From an overhead perspective, the line of the cabinets resembled a slithering snake, another element in Marshall's effort to carry the swooping features of the yacht's exterior to the interior.

"What I want to create is an informal space, something that feels more like an elegant hotel cocktail lounge than a nightclub," Marshall explained. With that in mind, he had placed a grand piano and a card table near the center of the room, and there were no large sofas or built-in furniture. Rather than having wood paneling on the walls, he proposed covering them with padded leather. "I would like to make this room different from everywhere else—spunky, funky, but also swank," Marshall said.

"If we're going to do something different, it makes sense to do it in the sky lounge," Von Allmen agreed. "But it has to be a soft and comfortable space because that's where we are going to spend most of our time." Von Allmen was not committing to anything—he would have a chance to react to a further-developed concept later on—but for now, Marshall had all the encouragement he needed.

With that, the meeting was over. For the most part, the Von Allmens liked what they had seen. There were negatives at every stage, but they were mostly quibbles. The positives clearly had won out. Marshall was elated, like an athlete who had just won the big game, but the presentation had exhausted him in a way that no one else in the room could understand. It was not yet noon, but as he stood up from the table and gathered the drawings, he said, "I feel like I need a gin and tonic."

7

Free Fall

There is nothing more enticing, disenchanting, and enslaving than the life at sea.

—*Lord Jim,* Joseph Conrad

For several decades following the Great Depression, large yachts became an endangered species, and by early 2009, Von Allmen worried that *Lady Linda*'s birth might coincide with the start of a similar trough. Given that he had always thought of his boats as a rarified kind of mobile home, his thoughts were further darkened by the devastation in real estate markets he heard about every day. Would big-time yachting also turn out to be a house of cards?

Florida has always seen more than its share of booms and busts, and Von Allmen regularly drove past empty buildings. The comparisons were all too easy to make. "People used to say the condo market in Miami was in solid shape because everything had been sold," he said. "But they did not see what really was going on: the condos had sold, but most of them were not owner occupied. The owners were speculators who could only afford to hold on to them if the market continued to rise. When the market fell apart, a flood of apartments were put up for sale, and there were no buyers except at fire-sale prices. The same thing could happen with yachts."

Von Allmen's personal financial concerns were intensifying. Following the sale of his companies, he had invested much of his wealth in stocks. During January 2009, the Dow Jones Industrial Average fell by 8.8 percent, the sharpest decline for that month in the index's nearly 112-year history, and Von Allmen knew the first months of the year often set the tone for the remaining ones. In February the Dow Jones Industrial Average fell by 12 percent, the worst performance for that month since 1933 and the sixth consecutive monthly decline. The market was less than half of what it had been in October 2007, and the Obama administration had announced plans to increase taxes and government spending.

Von Allmen said he was worried not only about his own finances but also by the direction in which the new president was taking the country. On February 27, a day after the federal government announced plans to acquire at least a third of Citicorp's stock to prevent the giant New York bank from collapsing, Von Allmen said, "A lot of people are unhappy about the wealth gap. They think we have to start socializing things. There's this mind-set now that anyone who has wealth is a criminal. It just scares me—not just for myself but for the country."

The yacht world's sky-is-the-limit approach to things had clearly come to an end. Builders were slashing their staffs, and some shut down entirely. Brokers estimated that more than 40 percent of the world's largest yachts—those 120 feet or longer—were up for sale. In addition to the altered economic realities, there was an emerging sense that excess was now undesirable and that giant yachts might even be seen as symbols of what had gone wrong.

Von Allmen was also worried about the viability of Trinity Yachts. With a substantial backlog of orders, its owners said they could continue operating at full capacity for the next couple of years even if they did not sign up a single additional customer, but Von Allmen believed their thinking was fundamentally flawed—no different from the crazy logic that had underpinned the overinflated residential real estate markets in Miami and elsewhere. Trinity's customers, after all, could lose so much money that they would be unwilling—or unable—to continue building, regardless of the terms of their contracts. Some contract holders probably had to sell existing yachts to pay for the new ones. And customers who planned to pay for their boats with borrowed money might be unable to secure a loan. The flow of yacht-building credit had been choked off at least as quickly as other types of lending.

One of Trinity's clients, a Russian oligarch who was said to be a billionaire, stopped making progress payments for his yacht. Trinity was unable even to contact him. John Dane knew of other Russians who had disappeared, sometimes permanently, and he sent word to the yard that work on the oligarch's yacht should cease. A real estate developer who had built some of the Miami condominiums that Von Allmen talked about had also stopped making progress payments, so that project was down as well. Several customers had been slow in sending money to Trinity, and some of them warned that they might not be able to make it to the finish line.

Like elsewhere in the economy, the slowed movement of cash set off a chain reaction, throwing into reverse forces that had flourished during the happy days of easy money. With fewer dollars coming in the door, Trinity had attempted to reduce its expenditures, or at least slow their rate, stretching out payments to its outside contractors, pushing subcontractors to reduce their prices, and trimming its own labor costs by shortening workweeks. Trinity was also seeking to raise money through loans or by selling ownership in the company, and, inevitably, this led to rumors. Of the firm's twenty active projects, it was said that three, five, even ten had been abandoned. While the rumors were exaggerated, a dramatic change had occurred: just a couple of years after the company had scrambled to overcome Hurricane Katrina, its viability was once again open to question.

In this altered environment, Trinity's customers had become much more attentive to costs. For Evan Marshall, this changed everything. "For the first time in ten years, all of my clients are becoming financially sensitive," he said. "They want to find cheaper marble and use less expensive woods." They were also examining their contracts in search of ways to limit costs and to enforce their rights. While they used to be annoyed by Trinity's change orders and the costs they entailed, they generally paid them without asking too many questions. Now they challenged every cost increase and sometimes refused to pay. At every level, tensions were rising.

This was reflected in an email about *Lady Linda* that Marshall received from a Trinity executive named Paul Goedtel on February 3. Goedtel said the "designer drawings" should have been sent to Trinity fourteen months ago and that their absence could cause major delays. Marshall was furious. The reason he had not completed the drawings was that Trinity had not provided him with engineering plans and specifications that he had requested repeatedly. Marshall guessed that Goedtel's email was part of the blame game. Trinity had fallen behind in *Lady Linda*'s construction, and the designer believed the email was part of the company's effort to create a paper trail that would enable it to fault someone else. It was a game that required participation, so he immediately fired off a reply to Goedtel along with six other Trinity executives:

"How can you possibly say that when Trinity has not sent us a single technical drawing for this boat? We've not had a single answer to my numerous emails requesting technical information. Now all of a sudden the sky has fallen in after months of hardly any communications and you need our drawings yesterday?"

Trinity was in a bind—several of them, actually. Some resulted from the usual conflicts between its interests and those of its business-savvy customers, and the balancing acts required to run so many large projects simultaneously, but economic hardship had made everything more complicated.

For example, a wealthy Arab businessman, who had commissioned Trinity's biggest project ever, a 242-footer, told Evan Marshall, the giant vessel's designer, that he would no longer pay *any* price increases that went beyond his contract price. One year earlier, Trinity had encouraged him to commit to spending $10.3 million for the interior woodwork—the paneling that would cover most of its walls and the built-in furniture—which would be provided by a New Zealand company called Robinson Marine. The amount was substantially more than what had been budgeted originally, but Trinity told him there was so much demand for top-quality wood-work that he had no choice. Marshall's client, who owned a company that manufactured chocolate-based products (his boat would be called *Cocoa Bean*), had agreed, but now that the superheated demand was gone, he told Marshall he was no longer comfortable with the arrangement.

Trinity had never done its own woodwork. John Dane believed the primary reason American yacht builders failed to compete with the legendary Dutch and German shipyards was the difficulty of replicating European craftsmanship. Adopting a strategy of if you can't beat them hire them, Trinity contracted overseas firms to do the woodwork. Some were based in Europe; others were in New Zealand and Australia, which had apprentice programs that produced highly skilled cabinetmakers. Companies there turned out work almost as good as those in Europe but at substantially lower costs.

Cocoa Bean's owner was also aware that the value of New Zea-land's currency had sunk relative to the American dollar, so he argued that his cost in American dollars should decline as well. Told that he was obligated to pay $10.3 million regardless of currency swings, he became even angrier, and he demanded that Trinity either negoti-ate a reduction or find a different contractor. Saying that they had already signed a contract that was denominated in US dollars, Trin-ity executives claimed they could not do anything. Marshall's client refused to accept that and he said he was so furious that he might halt construction altogether. Marshall was horrified by the possible loss of his biggest project. And so when his client asked him to solicit other bids for the woodwork, Marshall agreed. A few weeks later, a highly regarded Australian yacht builder, Azzura Marine, told him that it could do the work for $8.6 million.

Trinity executives were infuriated when they learned that Marshall had solicited an alternative bid. Jim Berulis, the Trinity executive who was responsible for the construction of yacht interiors, phoned Marshall and told him that Trinity had already signed a contract with Robinson.

"But you have the owner of a ninety-million-dollar project who is going to walk," Marshall replied, citing the approximate cost of building *Cocoa Bean*. "Why aren't you bending over backward to help him?"

To complicate matters further, Azzura had also become the leading candidate to build *Lady Linda*'s interior. Even if Trinity could get out of its contract with Robinson Marine, Berulis did not think the relatively small company had the capacity to handle such an important component for both projects.

ALTHOUGH VON ALLMEN knew nothing about *Cocoa Bean,* he did know that Azzura had agreed to a price of $5.9 million to fabricate and install *Lady Linda*'s woodwork, which made it the lowest of several bids. That amounted to $1,047 for each of the 5,656 square feet of interior space that would be used by the Von Allmens and their guests. By comparison, DWH, the German company that had done the woodwork for *Linda Lou,* his 197-footer, had bid $12.6 million, or $2,220 per square foot, and an Ohio-based company had bid $9.7 million. On the basis of the numbers, Von Allmen told Marshall he wanted to hire Azzura. This decision confirmed Von Allmen's changed approach to the building of his new boat: prior to the economic crisis, he had said he wanted DWH to build *Lady Linda*'s interior as part of his goal of creating the finest yacht in American history.

Because Trinity had never worked with Azzura before, Berulis flew to Australia to meet the company's management team and see its production facilities. He was impressed by what he saw but remained convinced that it could not take on two large interior projects. Once he returned to Gulfport, he told Marshall that Azzura could not do *Cocoa Bean*'s interior but that Robinson Marine had agreed to reduce its price somewhat. But while that freed Azzura to do *Lady Linda,* in mid-February Berulis told Marshall he had identified another problem: the woodwork depicted in the renderings that the designer had shown the Von Allmens at their apartment a few months earlier was much more elaborate than what was anticipated under Von Allmen's contract.

Much of the wood to be used was burl wood, highly figured timber that develops in sections of trees suffering from some form of environmental stress. Often triggered by mold or insects, it is something like cancer in that it causes abnormal and unusually rapid growth, which frequently manifests as a rounded outgrowth protruding from a trunk or limb. Relative to normal timber, the grain of burl wood is misshapen, but given its striking appearance, it has long been sought after by furniture makers. Because it is rare, it is also expensive. In addition, all of the surfaces were designed to have high-gloss finishes, which require tremendous amounts of labor. If Von Allmen wanted that kind of woodwork, Berulis told Marshall, the cost of building *Lady Linda* would increase by several million dollars.

"I don't think so," Marshall declared, noting that he had sent renderings showing his plans shortly after his meeting with the Von Allmens.

Marshall was worried about how Von Allmen would react to a request for more money, and he was also anxious about his own company. Five of his clients had yachts under construction. Although none of the owners seemed likely to stop work, he knew that could easily change. And it did not look as though there would be any new projects anytime soon. Sitting in his office late one afternoon, he said, "This could be the end of the era of humongous builds." In truth, there was a part of him that had always been uncomfortable with the extraordinary wealth that had propelled his professional life. He loved his work and did not want to design anything else, but he was politically liberal and an ardent supporter of President Barack Obama. "People are still going to want to have boats," he said. "But maybe we will go back to more reasonably sized yachts."

In February 2009 Marshall flew to Miami for the annual boat show there. One of the most popular exhibition areas was a new one: the "Affordability Pavilion," which showcased smaller, relatively low-cost boats.

Billy Smith, Trinity's chief salesman, had come to the show. Better than anyone, he knew how bad things were, but, as always, he was doing his best to put an optimistic spin on things. Anything else would only make matters worse. He declared that no Trinity yacht had ever been resold for less than its initial sale price and that the value of yachts had not declined as much as the stock market. "And with a boat," he added, "at least you can say you had some fun."

But optimism was otherwise in short supply. The industry executives who had been ebullient in Monaco a year and a half earlier were now sharing war stories. When Marshall visited Von Allmen at his house after the show one day, Von Allmen offered a realistic but better-than-doomsday assessment of where things stood. He said that only three of Trinity's projects had been abandoned. Even if there were more casualties, he was confident about the company's ability to complete *Lady Linda*. He had heard recently that Trinity was in serious discussions with an investor who might buy an interest in the company. And even if Trinity were to go bankrupt, he believed it would do so under chapter 11 of the federal bankruptcy code, which would enable it to continue operating while it worked to establish a more stable financial footing.

The following day, when Marshall returned to the boat show, he was surprised to learn that Von Allmen's 157-foot Trinity had been listed for sale with an asking price of $29.5 million. Von Allmen had also gone back on his longstanding vow that he would never charter his yachts. Just one year earlier, when one broker after another told him that *Linda Lou* could be rented out for $700,000 per week, Von Allmen had regularly turned them away. He and Linda did not want to remove their belongings from drawers and closets, and they did not like the idea of anyone else sleeping in their bed. Now that this seemed like an unaffordable extravagance, Von Allmen asked brokers to begin soliciting charters. They hoped to charge $495,000 per week, but there were no takers.

Marshall could not help but worry about what the altered economic realities would mean for *Lady Linda*. A few days after the show in Miami, he became particularly concerned. He had sent a revised set of renderings to Von Allmen, who responded with an uncharacteristically testy email: "I think the lighting plan is terrible. All it does is bathe everything in excessive light. It is going to be like walking into a grocery store where there is no ambiance as opposed to a high-end shop where a mood is created with the lighting. There needs to be bright areas on the features and darker areas in between. If your design group cannot do this, then we need to get someone who can."

While Marshall was not troubled by Von Allmen's specific complaints—he thought the problem was with the renderings, not with what they depicted—the email's tone was worrisome. If it was a sign of things to come, completing *Lady Linda* would become much more difficult.

8

Righting the Ship

The pessimist complains about the wind; the optimist
expects it to change; the realist adjusts the sails.

—WILLIAM ARTHUR WARD

IN MARCH 2009 the interior of the engine-room module Gale
Tribble had begun piecing together more than a year earlier still
did not look like it had anything to do with a boat. But now it and
the other boxlike assemblies comprising the hull had been joined
together except for the bow section, which would be attached
later. All of them had been built upside down, and they were still
oriented in that way when they were welded together. The next step,
scheduled for April 3, was to turn what hull there was upright. Given
its size, this was no small task. Even without the bow, *Lady Linda* had
grown to 165 feet in length. The weight was also substantial, about
eighty-five tons.

It had taken thousands of hours of labor and more than seven
thousand pieces of aluminum to get this far. Subsequent stages
would require much greater amounts of labor, and from a variety
of tradesmen. With so many things going on at the same time, the
process would become increasingly frenetic and complex. Progress
would be accelerated further by the installation of components that

had been manufactured elsewhere. But the rollover, as it was called, represented a significant milestone. Most of Trinity's yachts were completed one year after they were inverted.

On the last day of March, a low-riding, flatbed trailer capable of carrying 640 tons on its sixty-four rubber tires was driven into the yard and maneuvered into position beneath the hull, which had been raised above the floor by the travel lift. Once the hull was lowered onto pressure-treated blocks of wood that had been arranged on the trailer, it was rolled out of the shed and into another structure, the "paint shed," where every exterior and interior surface would be sandblasted and given a base coat of gray paint. As the upside-down hull emerged from the shed, it looked something like a wingless version of the Space Shuttle. A closer inspection revealed that the outside surfaces were far from smooth. The welds that joined the "shell plates" of the hull were clearly visible. The welding lines where modules had been joined to one another were even more pronounced.

The essentially flat surface that would become the floor of the main deck contained no openings to accommodate stairs, vents, pipes, and wires. It made more sense to hold off on creating any gaps that might allow construction debris to fall from one level to another. The one opening in the deck that did exist was a large one that revealed the interior of the engine room, and this would make it possible to install a pair of massive engines. One day after the hull entered the paint shed, the same opening allowed several men, who were wearing full-body protective clothing and masks, to climb inside to do the interior sandblasting and, the next day, to spray paint the same surfaces. When they were done, it was still possible to see the slender frames that Tribble had put into place, but now that they were gray and part of a much larger structure, they looked much more substantial.

On the morning of April 3, the sixty-four-wheel trailer carried *Lady Linda* outside to an open area where it was surrounded by three powerful cranes. One of them was positioned directly in front of what would become the bow. It held a five-inch-thick steel cable that was attached to a hook that had been welded to the hull. When the hull was lifted from the trailer, this cable would carry some of the boat's weight and also allow it to pivot during the rollover. The other two cranes, which were stationed on either side of the hull, about two-thirds of the way from the bow, would actually do the turning. Each of those cranes controlled a cable that would be attached to a hook that had been temporarily affixed to the opposite side of the hull. Several of the yard's burliest workers struggled against the weight and rigidity of one of the cables as they lugged it from one of the cranes, carried it underneath the hull, and then connected it to a hook on the other side. Another cable was taken over the top of the hull and attached to the other hook.

The strategy for the rollover was relatively straightforward. First, the three cranes would reel in their cables so they would grip the hull and lift it several feet above the trailer. Then the crane on one side of the vessel would begin to wind in its cable while the crane on the opposite side released the cable it controlled. As long as the movement of the cables was in sync, the hull would turn gently. But although the methodology was logical—akin to winding up and releasing, very slowly, a child's top—the scale of everything made it seem unlikely to succeed. Metal-crunching disaster seemed more likely.

No one was standing anywhere near the hull when the process began, and everyone was wearing hardhats—not that they would make any difference given the forces at play. As the cables pulled upward and began to take up the hull's weight, a nightmarish symphony of screeching arose. But by the time the hull was a few feet above the trailer, the cables had found more certain holds, and the only noise was the cranes' throaty diesels.

When the actual turning motion commenced, it was so slow as to be almost imperceptible, but then it accelerated somewhat. The movement was steady and smooth, and less than five minutes after the start of what presumably would be the hull's only inversion, it was complete. Once the wood blocks on the back of the trailer were rearranged to cradle the right-side-up hull, it was lowered. A couple of hours later, it was moved back into the yard and positioned not far from another metal assembly that had been under construction for several months. Almost as long as the hull, it was the first level of *Lady Linda*'s superstructure: the shell that would surround its main deck. A bit farther away stood a third construction. Less substantial than the other two, it was the uppermost part of the superstructure: the level that would contain the sky lounge and the bridge. Eventually both of the forms would be lifted and moved so they could be married to the rest of the yacht.

VON ALLMEN did not go to Gulfport to watch the rollover. He understood that it was an important marker on the road to *Lady Linda*'s completion, but for him the primary importance of the achievement was financial: a contractual requirement that he send a large progress payment to Trinity.

Meanwhile, in view of the continuing bad economic news, he was taking heretofore unthinkable steps to curtail his lifestyle expenditures. For the first time since he owned *Linda Lou,* Von Allmen had decided that it would not go to Europe for the summer. He had also agreed not to use his 157-foot Trinity while it was being marketed. In truth, he thought a sale was unlikely. "The problem," he said, "is that everyone thinks they are going to find someone so desperate that they will sell for fifty cents on the dollar."

But two weeks after the rollover, a serious buyer did emerge. John Staluppi, a flamboyant Florida-based car dealer, persuaded Von Allmen to accept $21 million. Although that was far lower than the $29.5 million asking price, it was equal to what Von Allmen had paid for the boat, so he would not suffer a loss. As part of their agreement, Staluppi would pay the brokerage commission. Yacht brokers' rates are theoretically set at an amount equal to 10 percent of the first $10 million of the sale price, 5 percent of the next $10 million, and 2.5 percent of anything above that—but the amount is negotiable. Since the brokerage firm, International Yacht Collection (better known as IYC), was a wholly owned subsidiary of Trinity and Von Allmen was funding one of Trinity's biggest ongoing projects, a solution seemed likely. But the broker insisted on a commission that Staluppi must have considered excessive, and he ended up withdrawing his offer.

ONE OF the people who watched the rollover was Gale Tribble. The production floor was not nearly as loud or as busy as it had been a few months earlier, in part because it was Friday, and many of his colleagues no longer worked on that day. As a result, the atmosphere was different. Alarms indicating that the overhead lifts were in motion still sounded, but not nearly as frequently as they had a few months earlier. And the machine that used to cut sheets of marine-grade aluminum into frames and other components twenty-four hours a day was idle.

The impact on Trinity's employees was substantial. Most of them continued to put in four ten-hour days Monday through Thursday, but many had been told not to come in on Friday for the eight-hour overtime shift. Given that they were paid time and a half for that shift, it amounted to a substantial reduction in their compensation: from fifty-two hours of pay to forty.

Sitting in his office not far from the yard, Billy Smith admitted that Trinity's backlog of orders, which had seemed so formidable a year before, was no longer sufficient. If the company did not line up some new contracts within the next few months, Smith said its future was doubtful. Down the hall, other Trinity executives were looking into the possibility of building high-speed vessels for military customers and the oil and gas industry. "We will chase anything we can to keep our workforce together," Smith said. "This thing we're in is another hurricane; our goal right now is to survive."

9

Never Enough Space

Now bring me that horizon.

—CAPTAIN JACK SPARROW IN *PIRATES OF THE CARIBBEAN*

WAYNE FRIERSON was working in a corner of *Lady Linda*'s engine room, two steps up a ladder so he could reach the ceiling. It was hot and incredibly noisy. High-speed electric saws were severing metal pipes and plates, and other pieces of metal were being hammered, almost constantly, so it was like being inside an oversized drum. Several other men also were at work there. All of them were wearing earplugs, but conversation would have been virtually impossible even if they were not.

The engine room would be the beating heart for all of *Lady Linda*'s mechanical operations. The air-conditioning system's five compressors, each with fifteen tons of cooling capacity, were lined up next to each other near the front. Frierson was getting ready to connect them to inch-thick copper-nickel pipes that would carry chilled water to thirty-six "cold coils": tightly wound swirls of pipe that would be positioned strategically throughout the vessel. Fresh air would be blown through the coils to produce cool air. Another set of copper pipes would recycle the no-longer-so-cold water back to the compressors. *Lady Linda* would ultimately have two and a half miles of pipes, amounting to seventy times its length, but the air-conditioning system would require more of Frierson's time than anything else.

Frierson was a pipefitter. At thirty-nine, he was a square-jawed, sturdily built man with a head of thick dark hair and a slender moustache. At the moment, he was rigging hangers that would hold the copper pipes until they could be connected permanently. Precision was critical. He needed to leave enough space for the insulation that would be wrapped around the chilled-water pipes to prevent them from dripping with condensation. But he could not let them take up too much space. Other kinds of pipes also had to be packed tightly near the ceiling to avoid intruding on the space below, and it seemed like the engineers who laid out the plans for the pipes never left enough room. Every half hour or so, he shot a laser beam near the ceiling to ensure that everything was high enough to provide the six feet ten inches of headroom required by Von Allmen's contract.

Before he started on the air-conditioning system, Frierson had worked on several other kinds of pipes, beginning with the ones that would remove water from the bottom of the hull and carry it overboard. After that, he installed a system that would take water in the opposite direction: from a pair of eighteen-inch-diameter holes that had been cut through either side of the hull about two feet below what would be the water line, Frierson arranged pipes that would bring seawater to cool the giant diesels and their exhaust. He also created a network of stainless-steel pipes linking the engines to five fuel tanks. Their combined capacity of twenty-two thousand gallons was enough to fill an average-sized swimming pool.

Installing the air-conditioning system's pipes would consume several weeks. Once they were done, he, with help from other fitters, would arrange pipes that would carry various types of water: potable (to faucets), "black water" (away from toilets), "gray water" (from sinks, showers, and washing machines), fire-protection-system water (to sprinklers and hoses), and the water that would be evacuated from deck drains. Still other pipes would carry lube oil, hydraulic fluid, and engine exhaust.

On commercial and military vessels, pipes are left exposed and clearly labeled according to their purpose and the direction of flow to facilitate maintenance and repairs. The priorities are different for yachts. One way to think about their interior is as unobstructed volumes of space, so hiding pipes from view—and minimizing the space they take—is paramount. This was reflected in Trinity's engineering documents: areas given over to pipes and other systems were described as "negative space."

The engine room was the hub for most of the pipes, and it was where Frierson spent most of his days. He was in a corner Doug Von Allmen was unlikely to ever see, but Frierson recognized the ultimate value of his work. "Space is what you're buying in these boats," he said during a break. "The better I am at my craft, the more space the owner can have."

Lady Linda required more than two and a half miles of pipes.

⋆

FRIERSON COULD not remember a time when he wasn't working. He grew up in Picayune, Mississippi, on a large farm that belonged to his grandfather. When he was very young, he carted feed to cattle and chicken. Later on he cut hay and timber, and butchered cattle. "The work never stopped," he said. "By the time I was eighteen, I was ready to retire."

Sports were his only relief and the only excuse from work his parents would accept, so he signed up for almost every school team: track, baseball, basketball, soccer, football. In 1986 he played receiver when Picayune High School's football squad won the state championship, and the University of Southern Mississippi gave him an athletic scholarship. But Frierson was unprepared for campus freedoms: after his girlfriend became pregnant, he lost his scholarship. They later married, but divorced after he joined the army and it became clear that he would be stationed in Germany.

Having always been good with guns—he tried to pick acorns off fence posts with a BB gun when he was just five and later won marksmanship contests—Frierson was trained as a sniper. During the months leading up to the first Iraq War, he was sent to Saudi Arabia. From there he made regular forays into Iraq to help guide cruise missiles to their targets. The method was outlandish but effective: a Chinook helicopter carried Frierson and a Datsun sedan into the desert. He could not speak Arabic, but he had grown a beard and dressed like the locals. Once he found a preassigned target from a map, he "painted" it with a laser beam and used an encrypted radio to signal the launch of a missile from a US Navy destroyer in the Persian Gulf. After the missile latched onto the laser and detonated into the target, generally just ten or fifteen minutes later, he called for a pickup, and he and the Datsun were lifted to safety.

A couple of years later, in 1993, he was sent to Somalia, where he was part of the disastrous military campaign in Mogadishu that was later described in Mark Bowden's book *Black Hawk Down*. Until then Frierson had claimed that butchering cows had desensitized him to death and killing, but his experience in Somalia was so horrific that he was unwilling to talk about what happened beyond saying, "It was a total mess."

After leaving the army in 1997, Frierson returned to the family farm with his second wife, a German woman he had met while stationed there. Rather than working as a farmer, he decided he would rather have a job that involved welding, a skill he had learned while repairing farm equipment. He worked for a shipyard in New Orleans for several years but left when he was asked to work the night shift, because the hours would have made it difficult to spend time with his now teenage daughter from his first marriage. In July 2006 he went to work at Trinity.

Frierson saw a connection between his work as a sniper and as a pipefitter: "I have always liked precision work. And when you organize pipes, you have to have a plan. You need to know where you're going to enter, exactly what you're going to do while you're there, and how you're going to get out. It's the same thing with being a sniper." Frierson's insistence on precision was also apparent in his personal grooming—his moustache, a sliver of hair just above his lip, was trimmed immaculately—and his aesthetic sensibilities. "I'm the kind of guy," he said, "who will walk into your house and start moving around the pictures if they aren't hanging straight."

THERE ARE two approaches to fitting pipes. One is based on eyeball assessments of what the angles should be as pipes reach from one place to another. The proponents of this method say they rely on instincts and experience. Others dismiss the technique as simplistic guesswork used by "stovepipe fitters" who do not understand mathematics. A more exacting method—the one Frierson generally used—requires algebra and calculus to determine lengths and angles. For him, the Holy Grail was the formulas contained in *The Pipe Fitters Blue Book*. Frierson believed his approach resulted in more efficient solutions and fewer mistakes; but although he kept a 1977 edition of the book in his tool kit, he rarely referred to it. He had memorized a few of the most useful formulas and had entered some of the others into a small notebook he carried in his back pocket.

Frierson frequently worked with Darren Richards, a pipe welder who was responsible for permanently joining sections of pipe that Frierson and other fitters placed and connected. Much of what Frierson and Richards said to each other would be meaningless to most people. At one point, Frierson said, "It's going to be a ninety-degree offset to a forty-five and then a roll pitch." Most of Frierson's work was unsupervised, although his productivity was monitored. Management knew how many hours he took to establish a given system of pipes and could compare that to the time it took other fitters. In addition, supervisors kept a tally on how much pipe Frierson ordered from the supply room, and that information could be used to gauge both his speed and how much pipe he wasted.

In spite of this, Frierson had the sense that he was his own boss. Trinity's engineering department had created detailed drawings for all of the pipes, but they were never entirely accurate. Before computers, precision had been even more difficult to achieve. In those days, each system was plotted on a sheet of Mylar film. With some boats, there were more than twenty pipe systems and as many Mylars, which were supposed to be held together against a light table to check for "interferences" among the systems. Computers made it much easier to combine the plumbing systems into a single visual and also to view them with a three-dimensional perspective. It was even possible to "fly" through computer-screen images to trace any given pipe from its source to its final destination. Each type of pipe was rendered with a different color. With such a representation, *Lady Linda*'s arteries looked absurdly complex: a futuristic rainbow of crisscrossing shafts of various colors and thicknesses, showing everything from the three-eighths-of-an-inch pipes that carried hydraulic fluids to the ten-inch conduits that would remove engine exhaust. But even with the enhanced level of precision this provided, perfection was a target, not an actual possibility. It was up to pipefitters to find solutions within the metallic reality of never enough space.

Frierson had folded and tucked into his shirt pocket a one-page plan showing how the chilled-water pipes were supposed to be threaded through the engine room, but he sometimes worked for hours at a time without looking at it. Tapping the pocket, he said, "This is only a basic plan, and it isn't always right. I have to make my own judgments."

EVEN WITH the largest of yachts, tugs-of-war over how much space should be dedicated to pipes and other systems were inevitable. Air-conditioning equipment, which requires air vents as well as pipes, is a frequent battleground, and it was also a particularly sensitive issue for Doug Von Allmen, who has no tolerance for any kind of noise. One of his biggest complaints about his 157-foot Trinity was the whistling sound he sometimes heard when the air-conditioning was turned to maximum strength.

Rob Shelnut, the captain of that vessel, and Ingo Pfotenhauer, a consultant who was monitoring the new boat's construction on Von Allmen's behalf, believed the new Trinity would have the same problem as the 157-footer because of what they believed to be the insufficient size of the air-conditioning ducts Evan Marshall had allowed for in his design.

On many yachts, major compartments such as the main salon and the sky lounge were designed with coffered ceilings, which made it possible to maximize the heights over the center of the rooms while leaving somewhat lower sections near the walls where overhead pipes and vents could be accommodated. But Marshall's design called for the same height—seven feet four inches—almost everywhere, which meant most of the ducts could be only four inches in diameter. While maximizing ceiling height was theoretically a good thing for Von Allmen, Shelnut and Pfotenhauer saw it as a job-endangering error. They thought the ducts had to be *six* inches in diameter. With that in mind, they met with several Trinity engineers on the same day that Frierson was installing chilled-water pipes in the engine room.

"It's like the Venturi effect," Shelnut said just before the meeting. "If the air moves too quickly, it's going to whistle; if the ducts are big enough, the velocity slows, and there's no noise."

The meeting took place in the engineering department's windowless conference room, where the walls were covered with schematic drawings of Trinity's current and most recent projects. "The air-conditioning is one thing the owner has always complained about," Shelnut told the engineers. "He is *very* sensitive to noise. If we don't get this right, he won't live with it. We'd have to do it all over again."

Brent Ashman, the engineer who was responsible for the air-conditioning system, listened politely. He had heard it all before. "This is not the only owner who is a noise freak," he said during a break. "Other boats are *much* more difficult. We have owners who keep their boats in the Persian Gulf, and we have others who want to go to the Arctic. It's the owners who want to take their boats to *every* extreme who are the real challenge." In dealing with boat owners and their agents, Ashman instinctively took the position that the customer was always right, and he understood why Von Allmen's representatives were concerned. "Three things matter to the owner: the exterior, the interior, and the air-conditioning," he explained. "The exterior has to look good, and the interior has to be perfect, but he isn't going to enjoy any of it if he has sweat on his brow." However, Ashman thought four-inch vents would be perfectly adequate as long as the airflow was balanced carefully. "It's true that velocity causes noise, but you can reduce it in other ways—and, by the way, you need velocity to spread cold air through a room so it doesn't just fall out of the vents like a waterfall." At least for now, though, Ashman had decided not to argue with Shelnut and Pfotenhauer.

When the meeting resumed, Mark Swanson, the chief engineer on Von Allmen's 157-footer, joined the discussion and introduced another air-conditioning requirement. He said cold coils had to be installed in the ceiling above the open-air space just behind the sky lounge in order to make outdoor dining there comfortable in otherwise excessively hot conditions. Sounding just like Shelnut when he spoke about Von Allmen's aversion to noise, Swanson said, "The owner is *very* sensitive to air temperature."

Air-conditioning outdoor spaces was not unusual on large yachts. But after Ashman identified points above the table location where chilled-water pipes could be channeled, he felt compelled to point out the obvious: "You have to remember that a breeze could take the cool air away." Swanson acknowledged this with a nod and then went on to describe the need for yet another set of devices that would enable the Von Allmens to spend more of their time in the natural world by creating an enhanced version of the real thing. For cooler days, he wanted to install heat panels, similar to the infrared heat lamps restaurants use to keep food warm, above the seats where the Von Allmens and their guests would eat.

Not a problem, Ashman said.

Once that was settled, Pfotenhauer and Shelnut returned to the topic of the air-conditioning ducts, and Ashman agreed to alter the plans to include six-inch ducts anywhere they were needed to prevent whistling.

After the meeting, Pfotenhauer said, "I don't think Evan realizes how serious the problem is, but he doesn't need to—we are going to fix it without him." Pfotenhauer had decided to tell Marshall about the changes through an email that did not invite comment or, for that matter, mention that some finished ceiling heights might be lowered. In a message he typed out a couple of hours later, he wrote: "Doug has experienced unacceptable A/C noise. To prevent this from reoccurring, the minimum ducting should not be less than six inches in diameter. Captain Rob and I have spoken to Trinity about this, and they will insure that the millwork package is planned so as to meet this minimum requirement."

Unaware that interior dimensions might be altered, Marshall made no reply, and in the end, the changes were minor. At a subsequent meeting, Ashman used a series of airflow calculations to persuade Pfotenhauer that four-inch vents would be adequate in almost every location.

10

Cash Crunch

Only two sailors, in my experience, never run aground.
One never left port, and the other is an atrocious liar.

—AUTHOR-SAILOR DON BAMFORD

As THE summer of 2009 began, *Lady Linda* was surrounded by uncertainties. Trinity had not signed up a new customer since the onset of the financial crisis, and the level of activity was continuing to slacken as existing projects were completed. Work hours were being curtailed further, and layoffs had begun. Gale Tribble and Wayne Frierson still worked their regular shifts, but Frierson, who continued to spend most of his time in *Lady Linda*'s engine room, had become so concerned about his employer's prospects that he was looking into other employment possibilities.

In the executive offices, John Dane was battling an array of problems, all of them stemming from a lack of cash. It was a drastic change. In the not-so-distant past, the flow of money was invariably positive: new customers were required to send seven-figure deposits when they signed their contracts even though construction would not begin for months or even years. And owners who believed their boats would be worth much more than their costs tended to make their progress payments on time.

Other than signing up new contracts and trimming its work-force, Trinity had just two immediate alternatives: delay payments to its outside suppliers or persuade existing customers to send more cash—if not by increasing the amounts or the speed of their progress payments, then by investing in the company or providing a loan. The cash crunch had become so pressing that Dane asked several customers if they would provide a short-term loan of $10 million, but he had yet to find any volunteers.

What little cash the company had was being rationed tightly, and even required expenditures were being choked off. Trinity was sup-posed to pay two $50,000 deposits for *Lady Linda* in June: one to the firm providing its navigational equipment and the other to the supplier of its audiovisual systems. Telling each supplier it could pay only $25,000 now, Trinity asked if it could pay the rest later. Both companies agreed, but even the diminished initial payments were slow in coming.

The most substantial contract was for *Lady Linda*'s woodwork. Back in January, Von Allmen had been told that Australia's Azzura Marine did beautiful work but had never done a yacht as large as *Lady Linda,* so the company stepped forward with a particularly attractive proposal. In fact, though, Von Allmen did not think the dollar amount had any relevance to him; he believed the cost would be covered as part of the base price in his contract with Trinity. Since then, however, it had become clear that something was not right, starting with Jim Berulis's telling Marshall about the need for a price increase, or what Trinity termed an "upcharge." In addition, Azzura had not sent the wood samples to Marshall and Von Allmen that they needed in order to select tree species and finishes. And Trinity's production managers were unwilling to tell Marshall when Azzura could commence its work or even if the two companies had actu-ally signed a contract. Marshall guessed that Trinity was holding off because executing the document would necessitate paying another deposit.

On July 1 Berulis ended the silence with a bombshell of an email. It said Von Allmen would have to pay an additional $1,650,426 to cover Azzura's work. In justifying his claim, Berulis said *Lady Linda*'s woodwork would be far more elaborate and therefore more costly than what was on Von Allmen's 157-footer. The comparison was important: according to his contract with Trinity, the woodwork of the new boat was included in the base price only if it was to the same standard as the previous boat's. Von Allmen understood that; however, given how aggressive Azzura supposedly had been in making its bid and the fact that no one had said anything about the need for an upcharge when he was first told about the bid, he assumed there would not be one.

Berulis presented a very different calculation. When the 157-footer was built in 2006, he said, its woodwork cost $4.7 million: $922 for each of its 5,909 square feet of interior space. Since the new boat would have 7,180 square feet of space, he argued that Trinity was obligated to cover up to $6.6 million of the cost. The email went on to say that Azzura would charge $8.3 million for the new boat (without explaining what happened to its original bid of $5.9 million). Subtracting the base price from $8.3 million, Berulis concluded, "The difference is $1,650,426."

Over the next couple of weeks, Ingo Pfotenhauer and Marshall learned that there was more to the story. Azzura had not increased its price, but its contract with Trinity had been denominated in Australian dollars—and Trinity did not sign the agreement until June 27. By then, the American dollar had plummeted relative to Australia's, and Trinity wanted to pass along the cost of that to Von Allmen.

These details infuriated Von Allmen. No one had told him that the $5.9 million amount was subject to currency fluctuations. Or that his base price was $6.6 million. And no one had told him that a currency loss had been locked in when the contract was formalized in June. From Von Allmen's perspective, there were several other problems with Berulis's calculation, not least the fact that the $922-per-

square-foot amount it assumed for the 157-footer's millwork was
what it had cost more than three years earlier. Marshall had told him
that the same work would cost more than $1,000 per square foot
now, which meant Berulis's base price was artificially low. Trinity's
calculation was a "smoke screen," Marshall said, designed to hide
the fact that Trinity was asking Von Allmen to cover the cost of the
sinking American dollar.

Marshall's greatest concern was *Lady Linda*'s design. If Von Allmen decided to alter it to eliminate the need for a cost increase, the
most distinctive elements would almost certainly suffer. Significant
savings could be achieved only by downgrading the quality of the
woodwork and replacing curved shapes with rectilinear forms. And
if it came to that, he said, *Lady Linda*'s interior would become "a glo-
rified cardboard box."

IN THE days of seemingly ever-rising yacht values, Trinity's customers often did not bother to challenge what the company called
upcharges. Two years earlier, another one of Marshall's clients,
Christine Lynn, was asked to pay an additional $2 million for the
woodwork in her 164-foot yacht, *Norwegian Queen*. Lynn, an insurance company executive and philanthropist, signed the paperwork
almost immediately after it arrived. A new, less forgiving tone had
been set by *Cocoa Bean*'s owner when he challenged the cost of his
yacht's woodwork. Marshall referred to this in an email to Von Allmen. "We had a bruising time resolving Trinity's attempt to add
extra costs," he wrote. "The battle left a lot of scars and put me in
Trinity's bad books, perhaps forever."

Hoping to keep out of the line of fire this time, Marshall encouraged Von Allmen to confront Trinity. In a July 23 email, Marshall
emphasized that all but $253,916 of the proposed upcharge for *Lady
Linda*'s woodwork resulted from the altered rate of exchange. One
day later, he pushed further: if Trinity expected Von Allmen to pay

more because of the difference in quality between the millwork on *Lady Linda* versus the 157-footer, he said the company should use "a valid, up-to-date" estimate for what it would take to replicate the previous yacht's millwork in the current market. In fact, Marshall had already obtained just that—an estimate from SMI Group, the New Zealand–based company that actually did the 157-footer's millwork—and its number was $1,080 per square foot.

Von Allmen was aboard *Linda Lou* for a cruise through the Great Lakes. Far less costly than sending the big yacht to Europe, it was his version of a stay-at-home vacation. A few hours after he received Marshall's email, Von Allmen tapped out a message to John Dane: "The proposed upcharge on the interior was a big surprise because I was told at one time that there was no additional charge." He went on to say he would like to see a "current quote" from SMI, without mentioning that Marshall had obtained one already.

When Dane replied later that day, he proposed an altogether different approach for eliminating the upcharge, suggesting that Marshall should "figure out how to make the boat less expensive to build."

Tough times or not, that was the last thing Von Allmen wanted to hear. In responding, he did not show the extent of his anger. He rarely did. Many years before, he had come to believe it was counterproductive to reveal his emotions, particularly negative feelings. "When you show someone you're upset, you let them control you," he said. But Von Allmen did disclose that he already had an up-to-date estimate. "I asked for a quote to build the 157-footer today, and it was way above the number Jim is using," he wrote. "If Jim has a quote he is using, I'll show you mine if you show me yours. This is only fair. I believe we have always dealt fairly with each other in the past. I would not want this to change my mind. Let's try and resolve this on a friendly and fair basis."

VON ALLMEN'S relationship with John Dane had always been complicated. Von Allmen admired Dane's career and liked him personally. He also understood that shipbuilding was a difficult industry, one that required large capital investments and was subject to potentially devastating fluctuations in demand. But Von Allmen also recognized that Dane was a tough-as-nails businessman and that what brought them together was ultimately a game of zero sums: a dollar more for Dane meant a dollar less for Von Allmen.

Their personal backgrounds were also very different. Dane, the eldest son of a successful New Orleans mortgage broker, was born in 1950 and enjoyed a privileged, upper-middle-class childhood. His connection to the water came early. He learned to sail on New Orleans's Lake Pontchartrain, and by age ten, he was participating in races at the venerable Southern Yacht Club. He also played a lot of baseball, but when time constraints forced him to choose between the two, he picked sailing because the combination of rules and tactics made it what he would later call "a thinking man's sport."

Unlike Von Allmen, Dane found success while he was still an adolescent, competing in junior championships on a variety of small boats throughout the United States and Europe. When he was eighteen, he qualified to sail in the trials that would select the Americans who would go to the 1968 Olympic Games. For the class of boats in which he was competing, he came in second, but only the top finisher earned a spot on the team. The top American went on to earn the gold medal.

Sailing led Dane to his career in shipbuilding. Always good at math, he enrolled at Tulane University to study engineering and stayed on to earn a PhD. Not long before he left school, he was at Southern Yacht Club when he met Harold Halter, whose Halter Marine Group produced vessels for the offshore oil industry. It was 1974, and soaring oil prices had resulted in a flood of new-build orders for Halter. He hired Dane to be a project manager, and his responsibilities expanded swiftly as the company turned out more than one hundred boats a year.

In 1988 Dane started a yacht-building division of Halter Marine with the help of Billy Smith, a childhood friend. Recognizing that the oil boom would not last forever, they thought diversifying into recreational vessels would protect them from the eventual downturn. Building large yachts was always the goal. "We didn't think it made any sense that Americans had to go to Europe to buy their yachts," Smith explained. After Halter Marine was merged into another company that had no interest in building pleasure crafts, Dane and Smith purchased that division and named it Trinity Yachts. The acquisition, which was completed in 2000, included the New Orleans shipyard that would be damaged by Katrina a few years later.

Their timing was superb. The great wealth explosion was fueling an unprecedented demand for boats. In 2000 the global population of yachts 80 feet and longer was about 2,000. By 2008, that number would soar to 3,800, and there were not nearly enough shipyards to keep up with the additional demand. And while Katrina had been a major challenge for Trinity, it had a silver lining. Prior to the hurricane, the company had booked so many orders that the New Orleans facility could not begin to keep pace. Dane had been thinking about expanding, and Katrina forced his hand. The sixty-acre shipyard he acquired in Gulfport, Mississippi, more than doubled Trinity's capacity. By 2006, the employee roster had broken one thousand, and the backlog of yacht orders, eleven before the hurricane, had expanded to twenty-four.

Dane continued to pursue competitive sailing at the highest levels. He made it to the Olympic trials in 1972, 1976, and 1984, each time just missing a place on the team. Dane refused to give up, and once Trinity had stabilized after Katrina, he decided that he would pursue his Olympic dream once again in 2008. This time he would team up with his thirty-year-old son-in-law, Austin Sperry, to compete in the Star class, a 22-foot keelboat. Dane would steer and Sperry would trim the sails. Certain that this would be his very last shot at being an Olympian, Dane set out to optimize his odds with what he described as his version of the Manhattan Project. He entered regattas around the world, and he hired sailing coaches, physical trainers, and a weather forecaster. All told, he invested $1.4 million in the effort—and it paid off. Almost four decades after his first Olympic effort, Dane and Sperry finished first in the trials. Just after the decisive race, he said, "I've been thirty-nine years close, and this is just an unbelievable end to a dream."

Once he arrived in China for the games in August 2008, Dane— who was, at age fifty-eight, the oldest competitor on the American team by seventeen years—was mistaken frequently for a coach. But after the first three races, he and Sperry were in first place. Then their luck ran out. Having studied twenty years of local weather conditions, Dane's meteorologist had concluded that the breeze at the Olympic sailing venue was generally light—less than ten miles per hour—and Dane's boat had been designed for those conditions. While that was helpful in the first races, the wind was much stronger during the rest of the regatta, and Dane and Sperry ended up finishing eleventh in a field of sixteen.

Dane did not linger to watch the rest of the Olympics. A couple of days after his final race, he was back at his desk, disappointed with the final result but already refocused on the future. "We took a bit of a gamble," he said, "and it turned out to be the wrong decision."

Von Allmen knew Trinity was in trouble. He was one of the people Dane had approached for a $10 million loan. Like the others, Von Allmen had declined, so he assumed Dane was still short of funds.

But his appreciation for Trinity's financial plight had done nothing to diminish his anger about the possibility of an upcharge for *Lady Linda*'s woodwork. On July 30 he wrote to Marshall to tell him that Dane still had not responded to the email he had sent a week earlier. Once again, Marshall sought to head off any thought of scaling back the boat's design. "We could of course downgrade a few features of the interior" for the woodwork, he wrote. "We could have less glossy finishes and we could reduce the use of burl wood, making for a plainer interior. But this might result in a maximum—and I'm guessing—$150,000 to $200,000 in savings, nothing like the $1.6 million the yard is trying to hit you up for!"

Von Allmen had no intention of reducing the quality of the yacht's interior finishes. Indeed, he was now inclined to go in the opposite direction because of the partial recovery of the stock market—and what he believed to be a remarkably lucrative investment opportunity he had learned about recently from one of his Fort Lauderdale neighbors. During the previous couple of months, Von Allmen had committed more than $70 million to the investment, and he believed it would throw off enormous profits in less than a year. This prospect had changed Von Allmen's attitude about everything. He was no longer thinking about selling *Linda Lou*. In fact, he had recently told its captain to make plans for taking it back to the Mediterranean for the summer of 2010.

Marshall became aware of his client's refortified sense of optimism when he met up with him at the Manhattan apartment to look at the wood samples he had finally received from Azzura. Von Allmen took particular interest in two of them: a veneer that could be used for the outside surfaces of a cabinet and a rounded, inch-thick strip of wood that could be used for the front edge—the bull nose—of the same piece of furniture. Both pieces were made from burled sections of a beech tree, but when Von Allmen held them together, he did not think they looked like they had come from the same timber. The mismatch would make the use of veneers obvious. It would look like a compromise, a cheap way out.

"Why can't we use solid pieces of wood?" he asked Marshall.

To construct burl-wood furniture without using veneers would cost at least $100,000 more, Marshall said, but with a wave of his hand, Von Allmen indicated that he did not have a problem with that.

ON AUGUST 10 Marshall traveled to Gulfport to meet a team of production managers from Azzura. The meeting was in the same windowless conference room where the discussion about *Lady Linda*'s air-conditioning system had taken place a few months earlier. It was in the building where most of Trinity's engineers had their cubicles, and as soon as Marshall passed through the front door, he noticed that many of them were no longer occupied. With no new boats to plan, engineering was inevitably one of the first departments to suffer.

The Azzura employees, all of them Australian, were already seated around the table when Marshall arrived. Their goal was to gather information needed to create the "shop drawings" that would guide the fabrication of the furniture and paneling. With spiral notebooks full of detailed specifications and questions for Marshall and Trinity's engineers, the Azzura representatives were obviously well prepared. At times they seemed to know the boat better than Trinity's engineers. For example, shortly after the meeting began, Craig Rothwell, the senior member of Azzura's team, pointed to a drawing and warned that a vent that would carry exhaust fumes from the galley might interfere with the mechanics that were supposed to move the panels that concealed the television screen in the Von Allmens' stateroom.

Rothwell marched through his questions about the specifications in excruciating detail: the direction of grains on doors and panels, the styles and sizes of moldings, the widths and depths of grooves, the shapes of the handrails, the type of frames that would surround paintings and mirrors, the locations of smoke detectors and recessed fire sprinklers, and the places where wall panels had to be removable to facilitate maintenance and repairs. Many of the issues were technical, but the discussion was also driven by the Von Allmens' desires. For example, Marshall said the closets had to be made from cedar and have a "strong scent" and that it was important to prevent any possibility of "creaking."

The cost of Azzura's work was unspoken until a break in the meeting when Rothwell pulled Marshall aside and asked, "Do you know what's going on with the exchange rate dispute?"

"I know there's been a problem," Marshall replied.

"Well, I hope the Von Allmens know that we have not changed our price," Rothwell said, obviously referring to the amount in terms of Australian dollars.

Not wanting to be seen as having a role in financial matters, Marshall nodded but said nothing further.

WHILE MARSHALL was meeting in the engineering department, Wayne Frierson was in *Lady Linda*'s engine room, working on the drainage system for the bilge. On most yachts, those pipes took about a month to install, but it had taken much longer with *Lady Linda*. Frierson understood why: in other projects he had worked on at this stage, there were about a dozen pipefitters, but he was one of only two on this one.

Frierson would not see *Lady Linda*'s construction through to completion. He planned to leave Trinity as soon as he received his next paycheck. He enjoyed the work, and several of his coworkers had become friends, but he was no longer willing to rely on Trinity for his employment. "It's become a dead-end job," he explained. "Everyone is walking on eggshells." He could not afford a reduction in pay, and being laid off when he did not have another job lined up would be even worse.

It was, he had decided, time for another career change. He had enrolled in a school that would train him for a health management position, and he had already lined up a job with a hospital in New Orleans.

FOLLOWING MARSHALL'S meeting with Azzura, Al Meneghin, Trinity's production supervisor, led the group over to the yard to see the *Lady Linda* itself. As soon as it came into view, it was obvious that something was terribly wrong. By now, the superstructure for the main deck should have been joined to the hull. But only a portion, the front half, had been attached. The odd form that resulted from this partial assembly did not look like a yacht. The abrupt end of the superstructure and flat-bedded rear half of the boat gave it the graceless lines of a cargo vessel.

Meneghin explained why: the engines had to be installed before the superstructure above the engine room was welded into place—it would be impossible to get them inside otherwise—and Trinity did not want to lay out the money for the engines just now.

The engines were a big expense. Under Von Allmen's contract, *Lady Linda* had to be capable of moving through the water at 20.5 knots, or 23.6 miles per hour. If its maximum speed was anything less than 20 knots, Von Allmen had the right to refuse delivery of the boat and was entitled to a full refund. Propelling a 487-ton vessel that fast would require two enormous engines, each of which would produce 3,384 horsepower. Together they would cost almost $2 million—and their manufacturer, Caterpillar, with lots of experience with the boat-building industry's ups and downs, never delivered an engine until it was paid for in full.

Cutting the main deck superstructure in half and joining it back together later had clearly required substantial amounts of extra labor. Since the only benefit was delaying the payment for the engines, Marshall worried that Trinity was running out of options. He also noticed that there were not many men working on the boat.

According to Von Allmen's original contract, *Lady Linda* should have been completed already. Alarmed by the latest developments, Marshall turned to Meneghin and asked, "At this point, when do you think the boat will be completed?"

"I can't give you a date."

"You must have an idea, right?"

"I don't know—I'm not supposed to know."

"So there is no real target date?"

"I didn't say that," Meneghin said. "I just said I can't give you a date."

Blinded by Thirst

Being rich means money is the only thing you don't
have to worry about.

—ATTRIBUTED TO JOHNNY CASH

EVEN AFTER Von Allmen began spending more time on the water
than in his office, he had never expected to retire fully. He had made
too much money. Determining how it should be invested was a job
in itself, as was managing his yachts and homes and their staffs. In
addition, the business of ferreting out moneymaking opportunities
had never lost its appeal. As the global financial meltdown continued,
he told friends he was thinking about "going back to work."

Then he met Scott Rothstein. A charismatic Bronx-born lawyer
who had recently moved into a house just down the street from the
Von Allmens in Fort Lauderdale, Rothstein described an investment
vehicle that seemed capable of not only recovering Von Allmen's
vanished wealth but perhaps even taking it to new heights. At first
Von Allmen had been reluctant. All of his most important financial successes had come from buying and selling entire companies.
Whenever he had strayed from the formula by investing passively
in other people's businesses, he had lost money. But Rothstein was

offering something different: an opportunity that was as peculiar as it was lucrative and that did not appear to involve a lot of risk.

Rothstein's own success had happened almost overnight. From a childhood that appeared to resemble Von Allmen's—Rothstein said his father had worked as an itinerant condom salesman—he put himself through college and then Fort Lauderdale's Nova Southeastern University Law School. While the early years of his legal career were undistinguished, in 2002, when he was forty-one, he founded his own firm. A few years later, Rothstein Rosenfeldt Adler had become a money-spinner, and Rothstein was a profligate spender. Indeed, even by South Florida's glitzy standards, his extravagance, which was unabated even during the depths of the financial crisis, set him apart. In addition to several homes, he acquired an 87-foot yacht, more than one hundred expensive watches—and a fleet of *twenty-five* automobiles that included two Rolls-Royces, a Bentley, a pair of Lamborghinis, four Ferraris, and a $1.5 million Bugatti Veyron.

High-profile charities and politicians, almost all of them Republican, were also among the beneficiaries of Rothstein's largesse. He and his law firm colleagues sent more than $100,000 to John McCain's 2008 presidential campaign. Florida's governor, Charlie Crist, was so grateful for Rothstein's cash that he invited him to help blow out the candles on his fifty-second birthday cake.

Money was a singular obsession, as Rothstein readily admitted. He attributed it to his childhood. "I grew up poor—I am a lunatic about money," he told Bob Norman, a reporter for the *New Times Broward–Palm Beach*. Some people thought he was just plain crazy. With a brash speaking manner that incorporated nasal traces of the Bronx and an overabundance of "y'alls," he spoke so rapidly and changed subjects so frequently that others wondered if he was a cocaine addict or suffered from some kind of attention deficit or hyperactivity disorder. He certainly did not look like a lawyer. Five foot six inches tall and overweight, Rothstein wore colorful hand-painted ties and a pair of orange-dyed ostrich-skin boots. He sometimes strapped a pistol to his left leg just above the ankle.

Rothstein's office was also unusual. Separated from almost all of his colleagues by a locked door, it had access to a private elevator that went to a secured section of the parking garage, enabling him to come and go without notice. Anyone who wanted to enter the inner sanctum, where microphones and surveillance cameras were mounted to the ceiling, had to call ahead to request an audience and use an intercom to ask for the door to be unlocked. Those who were admitted found an alligator-skin sofa and an opulent shrine to all things Rothstein: letters of thanks from charitable organizations; photographs of Rothstein with McCain, Rudy Giuliani, and Arnold Schwarzenegger; and a painting of Al Pacino playing Michael Corleone in *The Godfather.* Three computer screens shared space on his desk with the Torah and a plaque that read: "A good lawyer knows the law. A great lawyer knows the judges."

Rothstein began most of his days with a business breakfast at the beachfront Ritz-Carlton hotel. At night, he frequently could be found at a restaurant on the ground floor of his office building: Bova Prime, an Italian steakhouse he partially owned. More often than not, he was unaccompanied by his second wife, Kimberly. They had met when she was working as a bartender at the Blue Martini, a cocktail lounge in the nearby Galleria mall. She was thirty-three when they married in 2008. Kimberly frequently complained about how little time they spent together, but they celebrated their first wedding anniversary by going to an Eagles concert during which group member Don Henley extended his personal congratulations from the stage: "I don't normally do this, but this goes out to Scott and Princess Kimmie on their one-year wedding anniversary." To secure the shout-out, Rothstein had given $100,000 to a charity designated by Henley. The drummer-vocalist then launched into one of the group's classics, "Life in the Fast Lane." To some, the lyrics seemed prophetic: "Glowing and burning, blinded by thirst / They didn't see the stop sign."

FOR MUCH of Von Allmen's life, Scott Rothstein was not the kind of person he would have spent time with, let alone look to as a source of investment opportunities. "He was *very* flamboyant," Von Allmen said after they were introduced by a mutual friend. "But everyone is a little weird, including me, so I have learned not to judge people on first impressions. People I have started out liking have turned out to be scoundrels, and people who seemed like milquetoasts have turned out to be great friends."

Von Allmen also had an instinctive inclination to respect people who, like himself, had overcome difficult backgrounds to find great financial success. And he did not think Rothstein was crazy. "When he was with a group of people, he was completely over the top: bragging about his business, his cars, everything. But if you just sat down with him with less than four people, this persona of his went away, and he explained things in a calm, rational manner."

In early 2009 Von Allmen went to see Rothstein at his office, which appeared to be a substantial operation, with more than seventy attorneys. "Here, let me show you that we're no rinky-dink little law firm," Rothstein said as he invited Von Allmen to look over his shoulder at one of the computer screens on his desk. "I want to go online to show you that we have more than one billion in trust accounts"—money his firm had won on behalf of its clients and was holding for them in escrow accounts.

Then he explained how he got into the business of selling "structured settlements." It began accidentally, he said, after he represented a woman in negotiating a large award from her former husband. "The money was supposed to be paid out over nine months," Rothstein said, "but she didn't want to wait. She told me, 'I'll never see this money.' I told her it was going to be placed in a trust account and that there was *no way* he could get to it, but she wouldn't listen." Rothstein went on to explain that he could not receive his own fee until the matter was resolved: "Here I am trying to earn my fee, so I called a buddy and asked if he would buy the settlement at a discount. He said 'Sure,' and it worked out fine. It happened like that a few times. It was all informal. We didn't even put the agreement in writing. Now it's a real business."

In every case, Rothstein said the entire amount of the settlement was deposited into an escrow account from which money would be paid to victims over time, generally less than a year. The profits for investors who bought the settlements at a discount were always substantial: equal to at least 20 percent of their original investments.

Then Rothstein became more specific, describing several whistle-blower suits he was handling on behalf of employees of a large American company. "It's about a product being sold to the US government," he began. "I can't tell you the name of the company or what product it is, but I can tell you about a different case that's very similar. In that case, the government said it needed to buy a large amount of beef—one hundred percent beef—and someone gets the bid. Later on, this guy figures out he can make more money if he uses less beef, so he uses sixty percent beef, and the rest was filler. The company we're suing sells something else, but the circumstances are basically the same."

At that point, one of Rothstein's colleagues who was sitting in on the meeting used a stage whisper to interject, "Orange juice!"

Rothstein said he had gathered evidence that proved that the company told employees they would be fired if they told the government what was going on and that he then confronted senior executives, who agreed to compensate those employees for the illegal threats by paying each of them twelve monthly payments of $20,000. Since the employees didn't want to wait, Rothstein said, he sold the rights to the settlements to a friend for $100,000 apiece.

Von Allmen listened carefully. Although he was skeptical about some of the details, he accepted that Rothstein's story was possible. "I'm very free enterprise," he said later, "but I also know that crazy things happen when people sitting in corporate headquarters put out the word that you have to increase earnings by X by the end of the year or you're going to lose your job."

VON ALLMEN and Rothstein had common interests that went beyond their modest beginnings and their cars and yachts, most particularly their support for Republican politicians and their distaste for Democrats, especially Bill and Hillary Clinton. In a subsequent meeting, Rothstein told Von Allmen about several lawsuits his firm had initiated against Palm Beach billionaire Jeffrey Epstein, a Clinton supporter who was imprisoned after he pled guilty to charges that he had solicited prostitution.

Rothstein said investigators working for his firm had discovered that there had been incidents beyond the one that landed him in prison. Some of the offenses, Rothstein suggested, occurred aboard Epstein's private plane, a Boeing 727, possibly when the former president was on board. Rothstein showed Von Allmen what he said were thirteen boxes of case files, which included several flight manifests. Because of the threat of lawsuits, Rothstein claimed that Epstein had agreed to pay a total of $200 million in settlements to several young women. He would deposit the entire amount in escrow accounts, and the alleged victims would be paid out over several months according to the terms of a settlement agreement.

The delay in the payments gave rise to what Rothstein said was a spectacular investment opportunity: like the orange juice company employees, the young women did not want to wait and would happily accept substantially less money if they could get it immediately. It did not surprise Von Allmen that Epstein might be willing to pay so much money to eliminate the problem Rothstein described. He also knew legal settlements could be sold. However, the terms Rothstein described did not make sense. Why would the alleged victims give up so much in order to get their money less than a year earlier? And if the profits were so great, why wouldn't Rothstein put up the money himself?

Rothstein had a ready answer to every question. The girls were afraid that their well-connected assailant would find a way to avoid actually handing over the promised money, so they wanted to lock in what they could now. Rothstein said he could not buy the settlements himself because of the legal profession's conflict-of-interest rules. The alleged victims were emotional, Rothstein added. Even the discounted amounts were enormous, and the young women were desperate to put this behind them. In an email that described a settlement, Rothstein wrote: "It involves a horrific sexual assault against a girl that just turned 18. She was a minor when the attack occurred. She is giving up huge money, as she wants the attacker out of her life. She and her mom are moving the minute she gets her money."

Rothstein said Von Allmen's investment would be virtually risk free, and he offered up a host of assurances. Although Rothstein said the settlement agreements were confidential, he said Von Allmen could examine copies in which the names of the victims were obscured. He also said that TD Bank, a subsidiary of Canada's Toronto-Dominion Bank, would hold the escrow account, and it would provide a "lock letter" guaranteeing that the money in the escrow accounts could be paid only to Von Allmen. Finally, he could hire an independent "confirming agent" to authenticate the settlements and verify that Epstein's money had been deposited in a locked account.

"He had a logical explanation for everything," Von Allmen said later. "Everything seemed to make sense."

✳

THE DOUG Von Allmen who listened to Rothstein's pitch was demoralized. As in the early 1980s, when a recession and sky-high inflation had shaken his psyche so deeply that he stopped working, he found the drumbeat of dire economic news following the 2008 financial crisis so demoralizing that he had cut off his newspaper subscriptions. "I turn off the television when the news comes on," he said, "and I never listen to the radio in the car. I just try to stay away from bad news."

Von Allmen was so desperate for a positive story that his normal business judgment may have been impaired. He understood that investment returns that seem too good to be true generally are, but he thought Rothstein's settlements were such an unusual opportunity that they could not be evaluated in the normal ways. Ultimately, Von Allmen persuaded himself that the outsized returns were possible because of the special facts that were behind them as well as their obscurity. If the rights to the settlements were auctioned off, they undoubtedly would not be nearly so profitable.

In April 2009 Von Allmen hired Michael Szafranski, the man Rothstein described as the independent confirming agent (but who worked out of Rothstein's office), to substantiate that the Epstein settlements were legitimate and that the full amount of the settlements had been deposited into the accounts. Then Von Allmen invested heavily, utilizing a pair of trusts he created for that purpose: the Von Allmen Dynasty Trust and D&L Partners. During May and June, he wired $47 million to Rothstein's accounts at TD Bank. Linda's son and Von Allmen's stepson, Dean Kretschmar, invested an additional $8 million. Trusts benefiting Von Allmen's son and daughter-in-law, David and Ann Von Allmen, each invested $275,000.

Rothstein's business appeared to be booming, seemingly untouched by the financial catastrophes in the rest of the world. In a recent real estate buying binge, he had spent $17 million to acquire a

Manhattan apartment, two houses in Rhode Island, and an additional one in Fort Lauderdale. At the same time, though, he was apparently also becoming increasingly anxious about his personal security. In April he began paying off-duty police to guard him and his house in Fort Lauderdale, and the coverage soon expanded to include his office. "We will be providing special numbers to call in the event of security issues," he wrote in an email to the firm's employees. "You will see uniformed and plainclothes law enforcement present in our offices."

Rothstein also sought to heighten the already substantial barriers between him and his colleagues by discouraging them from visiting his personal office. "With the continued rapid growth of our firm, it has become more imperative than ever that our management team be given the time and space to accomplish all that they must accomplish during the day," he wrote in an August email. "Unless it is a true emergency, *no one* is to attempt to enter the admin corridor."

In September, Rothstein told Von Allmen about another investment opportunity: settlements he was about to conclude with Chiquita Brands International, the giant produce distributor, on behalf of a large number of plaintiffs. Once again, Rothstein said the payments would be made over time, and his clients did not want to wait. Von Allmen agreed to send $32 million to one of Rothstein's accounts.

The pace was accelerating. In early October Rothstein claimed to have negotiated a large settlement for the apparent victim of sexual harassment and discrimination, and he offered Von Allmen the chance to acquire six monthly settlement payments of $5 million—a total of $30 million—for $18 million. After Szafranski assured Von Allmen that another locked account had been established, he paid $13.5 million to secure a major interest in the settlement.

By mid-October 2009, Von Allmen and his family had handed over more than $100 million for Rothstein's settlements. The profits he expected to reap were so great that he was no longer trying to curtail his lifestyle expenses. When Evan Marshall told him that Trinity wanted to charge extra money for adding metal plates to the floor of *Lady Linda*'s sky lounge, where he was thinking about putting a baby grand piano, Von Allmen immediately agreed. Why not? By the end of the month, he believed, he would start collecting Rothstein's settlement payments. His anticipated profits—more than $35 million—were almost enough to cover the cost of building *Lady Linda*.

Pulling the Trigger

Should you find yourself in a chronically leaking boat,
energy devoted to changing vessels is likely to be more productive than energy devoted to patching leaks.

—WARREN BUFFETT

DURING THE last days of the summer of 2009, Trinity's cash-flow
crisis took a sudden turn for the worse.

Back when Von Allmen was negotiating his contract to build
Lady Linda, he had insisted that Trinity include a clause that enabled
him to return his 157-footer to the company once construction had
begun on the new boat. The arrangement was structured like the
trade-ins automobile dealers offer new car buyers, except that in this
case, the value of the older boat had been fixed in advance. And the
amount was very large: $21 million, or what Von Allmen had paid
for the yacht.

Back in 2006, Von Allmen thought there was little chance that he
would put the provision to use—he believed it would be worth much
more—but his long experience with buying and selling companies
had left him with an enduring appreciation for the importance of
thinking through every possible scenario and devising ways to protect himself from undesirable outcomes. John Dane had been reluc-

tant to provide such an option, but he did so because he was eager to sign Von Allmen for another project and because the clause did not appear to pose much of a risk. When the contract for *Lady Linda* was signed, on April 18, 2006, the 157-footer was almost complete, and Dane thought it would be worth at least $30 million.

The terms gave Von Allmen until September 30, 2009, to pull the trigger on his trade-in option, and he did so with just a couple of weeks to spare. Even with Scott Rothstein's lucrative investment opportunities, the logic for doing so had become overwhelming: in a rapidly declining market, he could unload a three-year-old yacht without taking a loss, and he no longer would have to shell out more than $2 million a year to cover its operating and maintenance costs.

However, because he would not be paid in cash, the transaction also carried risk. Von Allmen would receive a $21 million credit against the cost of *Lady Linda*. Since he had previously paid Trinity $5 million, he was now credited for having paid $26 million of the new yacht's base price of $37 million. If things went according to plan, it would be months before he would have to send any more money to Trinity. On the other hand, if Trinity went bankrupt, the value of Von Allmen's giant credit would be jeopardized. If it came to that, *Lady Linda* could still be completed, but it would be a messy process that would almost certainly result in further delay and additional costs. He would become one of the company's largest creditors and probably end up becoming one of its owners.

Dane was sitting at the round table in Von Allmen's New York apartment when Von Allmen delivered his news. Trying to ease the blow, he then said, "I don't know if it has occurred to you, but this could do a lot to help you solve your cash-flow problem."

On the face of it, it seemed like the exact opposite. Dane, after all, was being forced to accept ownership of a yacht that would be difficult, if not impossible, to resell—and he would have to perform $21 million worth of work on *Lady Linda* before its owner sent

Trinity another dollar. The company's cash crunch wouldn't ease, it would get worse. Much, much worse.

But Von Allmen offered a different perspective: "Once you own the boat, you could borrow a lot of money against it—probably ten million dollars."

FOLLOWING THE Great Depression, it took more than fifty years for large yachts to make a comeback in the United States. Of the big boats that remained in service, many belonged to the royal families of Europe. The monarchs of England, Denmark, and Norway have had floating palaces since the sixteen hundreds. Denmark launched a new 257-foot royal yacht in 1932 that remained in service for the rest of the century and beyond. Norway presented a 263-foot yacht to King Haakon VII in 1947.

King George V at the helm of his 122-foot racing yacht.

England, starting with Charles II's coronation in 1660, has had more than eighty royal yachts, including the 412-foot HMY *Britannia* that was launched in 1953. Commanded by an admiral, its crew of twenty officers and more than two hundred Royal Navy sailors communicated with hand signals so as to maintain the kind of tranquility the Windsors had come to expect in their homes. By the time it was decommissioned in 1997, *Britannia* had traveled more than one million miles and visited 135 countries. Queen Elizabeth II, whose coronation took place the same year *Britannia* was launched, said it was the only place where she could truly relax. At a ceremony marking its decommissioning, the generally unemotional monarch was seen shedding a tear.

Some of the largest private yachts after World War II were owned by Greek shipping magnates who capitalized on the dislocation of the postwar period. In 1947 Stavros Niarchos purchased a 214-foot, three-masted schooner, which had been stripped of its masts and most of its interior during the war. Following a meticulous refit, *Creole,* a narrow, black-hulled beauty, was adorned with museum-worthy paintings, mostly by van Gogh and El Greco. The world's largest privately owned sailboat, *Creole* added a new dimension to Niarchos's competition with Aristotle Onassis, his rival in business as well as almost every other aspect of life: women, the size of their private islands, and, starting in the 1950s, their yachts and the guests they attracted.

In 1954 Onassis bought a naval frigate from the Canadian government. He paid just $34,000, its scrap value, but after pouring more than $4 million into its remaking, the 325-foot *Christina* had amenities that would be talked about for decades: a medical clinic with a fully equipped operating room, a seaplane, and a large swimming pool. The bottom of the pool, a brightly colored mosaic that portrayed a young man leaping over a bull, could be raised flush with the deck to become a dance floor. Onassis did much of his entertaining in what became known as "Ari's bar," an intimate space in which the bar stools were upholstered with whale foreskin, a detail Onassis rarely failed to share with his guests.

Christina became a celebrity magnet. Winston Churchill was on board for eight cruises, and it was where the former British prime minister and John F. Kennedy first met. Other guests included Elizabeth Taylor and Richard Burton, Frank Sinatra, Greta Garbo, Marilyn Monroe, Rudolf Nureyev, and John Wayne. Sometimes called "the lust bucket" by its crew, it was where Onassis pursued the relationship with opera diva Maria Callas that cost him his marriage, and also the venue for two of the most glamorous weddings of the twentieth century: Prince Rainer III's to Grace Kelly and Onassis's own to Jacqueline Kennedy. "The great thing about a yacht," he said, "is that you raise anchor and then you tell the world to bugger off. It's pure freedom."

Eventually Niarchos decided that he too needed to have a large power yacht, and in 1973 he launched *Atlantis*. At 385 feet, its size easily outdistanced *Christina*'s. Niarchos's new toy also had a swimming pool, this one with a gyroscopically controlled system for calming the water when the yacht was in turbulent seas. Having made much of his fortune shipping crude oil from Saudi Arabia, Niarchos eventually gave the yacht to its crown prince, the future King Fahd. He then built an almost identical replacement, *Atlantis II*, which was completed in 1981.

Wealthy Arabs have had yachts since the pharaohs. In the 1860s Egypt's ruler built a 421-foot steam-powered paddle wheeler that was later lengthened to 478 feet and converted to propeller propulsion. It was the first vessel to pass through the Suez Canal and remained the presidential yacht all the way through Hosni Mubarak's reign, although he used it only rarely. Other Arabs were much more enthusiastic about their boats, in part because they provided luxurious havens aboard which the rigid religious restrictions of their homelands could be ignored without notice or consequence. For them, yachts were essentially private floating hotels and this was evident in their design: while most yachts had generous outdoor spaces for sun bathing and entertaining, the deck space on Arab yachts was generally limited. The focus was on large and lavish interior spaces.

The Saudis accounted for the mightiest fleet. During the late 1970s, Adnan Khashoggi, the Saudi arms dealer who was sometimes said to be the world's richest man, built *Nabila,* a 281-footer that was featured in the 1983 James Bond film *Never Say Never Again.* Five decks high, it had three elevators, a cinema, a billiard room, and more than 250 telephones. After Khashoggi encountered financial difficulties, *Nabila* was acquired by the sultan of Brunei and then by Donald Trump, who renamed it *Trump Princess.* In 1991 the yacht returned to Saudi hands when it was purchased by Prince Alwaleed bin Talal, the nephew of the king, best known for his investments in Citicorp and other major multinational corporations.

Not long after King Fahd received *Atlantis,* he contracted with a Danish shipyard to build a far larger yacht, which was completed in 1984. At 482 feet, *Prince Abdulaziz* was bigger than *Britannia.* It looked like an ocean liner, and for twenty-two years, it would rank as the world's biggest yacht. When Fahd died in 2005, it was inherited by his half brother, Abdullah, the new king.

The Saudis were not the only Arab owners of large yachts. In 1976 Libya's Mu'ammar Gadhafi acquired a 130-foot Feadship that spent much of its time in Malta. Iraqi strongman Saddam Hussein ordered a 269-footer that was completed in 1981, although he apparently never had a chance to step on board because of wars with Iran and the United States. Qatar's ruling family has had several yachts, including two that are longer than 400 feet and a pair of nearly identical 262-footers. The sultan of Oman built a 340-footer in 1982, which he later replaced with a 508-foot monster. A fan of classical music, the sultan outfitted the newer yacht with a music room large enough to accommodate a fifty-member orchestra.

But the Saudis remained the region's dominant yacht owners. Members of the House of Saud accumulated more than a dozen huge yachts. King Abdullah's half brother and the country's minister of defense, Prince Sultan bin Abdul Aziz, built a particularly large one: *Al Salamah,* a 457-footer with *eight* decks, eighty-two compartments, and a crew of ninety-six.

The Saudi yachts spent their time in ports in France, Spain, and Morocco, where they were unlikely to stir resentment at home. But they were too large and too eye-catching to go unnoticed. A 344-foot yacht belonging to Nasser Al-Rashid, an influential advisor to the royal family, earned a particularly unwelcome notoriety after it ran aground just off a popular beach in Cannes on a summer Saturday that coincided with the namesake film festival. The beach had to be closed, and newspapers around the world soon carried photographs of the awkwardly listing vessel as it was surrounded by barriers that had been set up to contain any leaking fuel.

UNTIL THE 1980s, there were very few really large American-owned yachts. Expectations had changed dramatically since the Roaring Twenties. In the 1960s, Henry Ford II acquired a Feadship that was 108 feet long, about a third as long as J.P. Morgan's last *Corsair,* but *Newsweek* reported on its amenities with a tone of breathless astonishment: "The chosen few have access to a 24-by-14-foot main salon, a dining room, five bathrooms, two bars, a television, an automatic washing machine and two speedboats."

No one did more to encourage big-boat ownership in the United States than Malcolm Forbes. For more than fifty years, he entertained corporate chieftains and advertising executives during cruises in New York Harbor and elsewhere. He employed a succession of five yachts, all of them named *Highlander,* each one larger than its predecessor. The first, which went into service in 1952, was a 72-footer. The last, a 151-foot green-hulled Feadship designed by Jon Bannenberg, was launched in 1985. From May until Novem-

Stavros Niarchos's *Creole* was adorned with paintings by Van Gogh and El Greco.

Aristotle Onassis's 352-foot *Christina* was a celebrity magnet and also known for barstools upholstered in whale foreskin.

(above) When the modern-day *Britannia* was retired in 1997, the usually unemotional Queen Elizabeth II shed a tear.

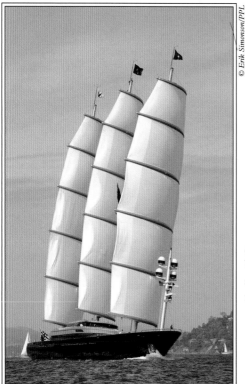

(left) Venture capitalist Tom Perkins built *Maltese Falcon*, a 289-foot-long schooner with masts that can be rotated to enhance its performance.

Linda and Doug Von Allmen.

To minimize labor costs, *Lady Linda*'s hull was built upside down— but eventually it had to be righted.

The vessel takes shape at the Trinity Yachts shipyard in Gulfport, Mississippi.

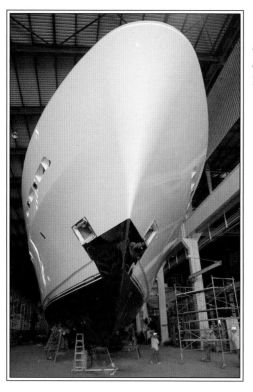

Once the fairing and painting were completed, *Lady Linda*'s arched bow had a lustrous sheen.

A $1.8 million lift raises the 487-ton yacht.

Lady Linda finally rolls toward its element.

Lady Linda's main stairwell was surrounded by a mythical scene based on artwork created for the SS *Normandie*.

With blue fabrics, silver paneling, and serpentine floors, the "sky lounge" has several seating areas and a bar.

An outdoor table where the nearby air can be heated and cooled.

The rounded shower enclosure in Linda's bathroom reflects Evan Marshall's taste for curved shapes.

Lady Linda's master stateroom.

The "sky lounge" is contemporary in style but has elements of Art Deco.

The uppermost deck, the "fly bridge," includes seating areas, a Jacuzzi, a bar, and gym equipment.

ber, drinks and dinner were served on board to 120 people three times a week. Some of Forbes's guests, among them Henry Ford II, went on to buy yachts of their own. Others, including a young Evan Marshall, were inspired by the mere sight of the lavish *Highlanders*. (When the Forbes family put the 151-footer up for sale in 2011, it was said to be a sign of the changed times and an inevitability, given the decline of traditional media; however, some said the sale would not have happened if Malcolm Forbes were still alive.)

Outsized personalities have often been the driving force behind exceptionally large yachts. Levittown creator Bill Levitt, one of the best known businessmen of his time, was a pioneer in both business and yachting during the postwar period. Having mass-produced thousands of cookie-cutter houses that he sold for less than $10,000, he was called the father of the modern American suburb and featured on the cover of *Time* magazine. Levitt was happy to admit that ego fueled his ambitions. "There's a thrill in meeting a demand with a product no one else can meet," he once told the *New York Times*. "But I'm not here to just build and sell houses. To be perfectly frank, I'm looking for a little glory." Levitt bought a 250-foot yacht shortly after he sold his company in 1967. Because of the vessel's size and the celebrities who came aboard for the Levitts' parties, it received widespread media attention during his ownership—and all over again after Levitt lost most of his money and had to sell the boat.

The other big-boat pioneer in the United States was Charles Revson, who started out selling nail polish in the 1930s and went on to create Revlon, the staggeringly profitable cosmetics-industry powerhouse. Aside from his company, he was best known for his difficult personality, his insistence on perfection, and his extravagance. In the 1960s, his lifestyle cost a then-unthinkable $5,000 a day, in part because of his 257-foot yacht, which had a thirty-person crew and a fuel tank that cost $20,000 to fill.

It would take another quarter century before American big-boat standards began to ratchet upward substantially. After Leslie Wexner led the way, it was Paul Allen's 414-foot yacht *Octopus* that set the standard. The $250 million vessel had an ice-rated hull to facilitate Antarctic explorations and a sixty-person crew that included several former Navy SEALs. Its garage had room for seven smaller vessels, one of them a tender so large—63 feet—that it might be considered a yacht in its own right. There were two helicopters and as many helipads, one at the bow and one near the stern, and a pair of submarines that could submerge through an unseen underwater hatch. One was capable of taking up to ten passengers for underwater explorations over extended periods of time; the other could be operated remotely in extreme depths. Reflecting the range of Allen's interests, *Octopus* also boasted a basketball court, an extensive collection of memorabilia from Ernest Shackleton's voyages to Antarctica, and a commercial-quality recording studio.

While *Octopus* became America's largest yacht when it was launched in 2003, another high-tech multibillionaire, Larry Ellison, had already taken steps to ensure that its reign would be brief. When *Octopus*'s construction was past the point where it could be altered, Ellison instructed Lürssen, which was building both yachts, to stretch the length of his *Rising Sun* from 393 feet to 452. Launched in late 2004, it had more than 85,000 square feet of living area and carried more than a dozen smaller boats, including a jeep-bearing landing craft. The mother ship was powered by four engines that together produced 48,000 horsepower.

Ellison admitted that his creation was a great indulgence. "It's absolutely excessive," he told *Vanity Fair* magazine. "No question about it. But it's amazing what you can get used to."

By 2005, Americans owned five of the world's twenty largest yachts, up from just one in 1985. The next tier down, propelled by people like Doug Von Allmen, included an even greater US representation. Most members of the new generation of American yacht owners were self-made entrepreneurs who were not inclined to adhere to yachting traditions. Jacuzzis and gyms became standard, and elevators, movie theaters, discotheques, and playrooms for children were regularly part of the mix. One of Lürssen's yachts had a "snow room," a compartment in which passengers could leap into machine-made white stuff following their saunas for a Nordic chill even as they cruised the tropics. Charles Simonyi, the Microsoft alumnus who created the company's flagship Office software applications, had his 233-foot yacht *Skat* painted with the battleship gray of a warship. Apple's Steve Jobs, during the months just before he died in 2011, was working with designer Philippe Starck to finalize plans for a large Feadship that would have the same sleek, minimalist lines and large panels of glass as his retail stores.

Even before the economic crash of 2008, there were some indications that the galloping advance of expectations was beginning to falter, and not just for financial reasons. Larry Ellison was annoyed that *Rising Sun* could not be accommodated in recreational marinas. In 2007, it went to Valencia, Spain, where he was attempting to wrest the America's Cup from Ernesto Bertarelli, an heir to a Swiss pharmaceutical fortune. Ellison's yacht was relegated to a commercial dock where it was surrounded by rusting freighters and stinking fishing boats. Meanwhile, Bertarelli's relatively modest 155-foot Feadship shared a dock with other yachts and was within shouting range of the racing machines that would compete for the Cup.

Rising Sun had another flaw. Because of its size and minimalist interiors, Ellison said it did not have enough intimate spaces. One of his guests put it more bluntly, saying, "It's like walking in an empty mall." Not one to live with a mistake, not even a vastly expensive one of his own making, Ellison sold *Rising Sun* to his friend David Geffen, the billionaire music and media entrepreneur. Although Ellison already owned a smaller yacht, a 192-footer that sometimes anchored within swimming distance of his beach house in Malibu, California, he contracted with Feadship to build a new yacht that had the same look and expansive windows as *Rising Sun* but was substantially smaller. Launched in 2011, *Musashi* was 288 feet long—by every standard but his own, enormous, but for Ellison, a significant downsizing.

A COUPLE of weeks after Von Allmen told Dane he was returning the 157-footer, Marshall arrived at the Von Allmens' house in Florida with another batch of wood samples from Azzura. One of the first things Von Allmen looked at was new pieces of the beech burl: a bull nose and a sheet of veneer. Since the last meeting, Marshall had learned that using solid beech burl rather than veneer would result in an upcharge much larger than he had estimated—$350,000—but he did not share that number with Von Allmen. He did not have to. After Von Allmen held the samples next to each other and tilted them so they captured the light in different ways, he concluded that they matched closely enough that there was no need to switch to solid burl wood.

Just before Marshall left the house, he told Von Allmen about his most recent visit to Gulfport, saying, "Your boat is looking a little odd right now."

"What do you mean?"

Marshall explained that the superstructure for *Lady Linda*'s main deck level had been carved in half and that only the front section had been mounted on the hull because Trinity wanted to delay paying for the engines. Von Allmen said nothing, but his facial features tightened.

13

Too Many Boats

I once knew a writer who, after saying beautiful things about the sea, passed through a Pacific hurricane, and he became a changed man.

—Captain Joshua Slocum, the first man to single-
handedly sail around the world (1895–1898)

The Fort Lauderdale International Boat Show, which takes place every October, is the yachting industry's most important marketing event. As the 2009 edition approached, Trinity was doing what it could to keep up appearances. It continued to buy premium advertising space in the major yachting magazines, and it had arranged to have an outsized presence at the show: While most of the other major yacht builders would make do with booths in the windowless "builders' pavilion," Trinity had its own floating hospitality center positioned near the middle of the most prominent dock. The glass-walled structure was furnished with overstuffed sofas and surrounded by seven of Trinity's recently completed vessels and watched over by a uniformed guard.

Billy Smith was a constant presence, and he never stopped talking as he greeted potential customers, brokers, and designers. Whenever he needed to free himself from one person to talk to the next, he arranged a yacht tour, some of them led by young fashion models who had been hired for that purpose. Smith did not deny the tough times, but his essential optimism was clearly unbroken. "Our customers are not going to change their lifestyles," he declared on Friday morning, the second day of the show. "They are not going to fly commercial—and they are not going to live without a yacht. It might not be a three-hundred-foot yacht, but they will have a two-hundred-footer."

Outside, the atmosphere was festive. The sky was blue, and a band was playing at a crowded dockside bar. According to the show's sponsors, it was the biggest ever, with more than $3 billion worth of vessels. Particularly impressive was the number of very large yachts: more than 150 with lengths exceeding 100 feet. The docks were crowded, and pedestrian traffic jams were frequent as families stopped to gape upward at the vessels that towered above them. Children asked their parents why they did not have a big boat, and their parents did their best to explain. Other high-end products were also on display. Several Ferraris were parked not far from the bar. Toy versions of the same cars were also available for $5 to $40.

Vehicles with such radically different price points provided a clue to an otherwise not-so-obvious boat show reality: there were actually two versions of the show, and their audiences were completely different from one another. Members of the larger group were essentially tourists: people who enjoyed looking at boats. The other, much smaller group included yacht owners and potential owners as well as the people who make their living serving the owners. It was not difficult to distinguish between the two. With unseasonably hot weather, the recreational visitors were dressed casually, most of them in shorts. Yacht owners and industry professionals wore long pants.

The two groups had very different impressions of what they were seeing. For the people in shorts, it was a festival of mind-boggling abundance, proof positive that either the great recession was not so great or that it had already passed. For industry participants, the show demonstrated the desperate state of things. They understood that the extraordinarily large number of big boats resulted from the fact that many of their owners could not afford to own them anymore. They had brought them to Fort Lauderdale because they wanted to sell them.

This reality was particularly apparent at Trinity. In previous years, the dock surrounding its reception center was filled with yachts that had been completed recently and turned over to their owners. Some of those owners agreed to display their yachts because they were proud of them; others did it as a favor, to help Trinity to sign up new projects. This year's crop was there for a different reason: *all seven were available for purchase.* One of them was the 196-foot *Bacarella,* the largest Trinity to date. Commissioned by a Russian oligarch and designed by Dicky Bannenberg, the son of the legendary designer (who died in 2002), its sleek interior had been received favorably by yachting publications, and Smith had hoped the vessel would go to Europe and assist his sales efforts there. But its future home was now uncertain because the owner had failed to pay for it in full; Smith was telling brokers it could be had for $65 million. Brokers recognized that something was amiss as soon as they saw that *Bacarella*'s gleaming white stern had not been painted to indicate the vessel's name or port of registry.

Almost no large yachts were registered in the United States, including those owned by Americans. There were three reasons for that, starting with "use taxes," state-imposed sales taxes that were imposed on boats built in the States unless they were registered abroad. In addition, any American-registered yacht weighing more than three hundred tons was required to meet the same safety regulations as cruise ships, which were generally considered excessive for private yachts. Finally, it was difficult for American-flagged vessels to employ foreign crew members when they were in US waters. As a result, most American yachts flew "flags of convenience," the most popular being those from the Cayman Islands, Marshall Islands, Bermuda, Channel Islands, and St. Vincent.

Following the global financial crisis in 2008, there were lots of sellers but almost no buyers at Fort Lauderdale's annual boat show.

THE VON Allmens' former boat—the 157-footer that now belonged to Trinity—was one of the seven yachts next to the hospitality center even though it had been completed three years earlier. It could have been displayed along a less prominent stretch of dock where several other older Trinities were being marketed by International Yacht Collection, Trinity's brokerage arm; but because Trinity was eager to sell it, it had been positioned next to the new boats. It was the equivalent of a car dealer taking a used vehicle from the back lot and moving it to the showroom up front. But even with special marketing, it would not be an easy sale. IYC was attempting to sell a total of fourteen Trinities. All told, more than a third of Trinity's global fleet was currently on the market.

More than anything else, that reality—too many boats for sale—was the real story of the show. As with the housing markets, the overhang of too much product was exerting so much downward pressure on prices that the market was not really functioning. What buyers there were demanded fire-sale prices. Those interested in building a new boat were an even rarer breed, and they expected to pay far less than what had been required a couple of years earlier. Seeing no alternative, some builders were attempting to buy time by offering prices so low that they seemed unlikely to even cover their costs. Billy Smith called them "kamikaze sales."

Builders and brokers acknowledged their predicaments with varying degrees of candor. Smith admitted that some of the existing Trinities would probably end up selling for less than what their owners had paid for them: "I have been telling owners that they might lose ten percent of their investment." But then, as always, he found a way to end on a positive: "When I tell them that, they say, 'That's okay—that would make it the best investment I have.'"

ON SATURDAY morning, Benetti, one of Italy's largest yacht builders, invited journalists covering the show to breakfast with several of its top executives. "Until this happened, my job was easy," Stefano de Vivo, the company's head of sales, said of the beleaguered economy. "I could just sit at my desk, and customers knocked on the door. Now, no one likes to say it, but we are in a crisis. Let's just say it: we are in a crisis."

Vincenzo Poerio, Benetti's chief executive, railed against the low prices for which some of his competitors were offering to build new yachts—the kamikaze sales. "These prices are unbelievable! They make no sense! We cannot sell at these prices. We have to become more efficient, but we cannot cut costs by so much."

De Vivo went on to describe a new line of boats the company hoped to build. Toward the end of his presentation, having seemingly decided that he had been *too* negative in his market assessment, he sought to backtrack a bit. "Actually, it's not so bad," he said. "We don't want to say we are not selling any boats."

"You don't have to; they know it," his boss deadpanned.

Further calibrating, de Vivo said, "Well, at least we are still in business."

Later that morning, two employees of Wisconsin-based Burger Boat Company, which described itself as America's oldest yacht builder, were sitting behind the counter of their booth. With no customers in sight, they were doing their best to talk each other into a positive frame of mind. "We've seen some really positive leads here, haven't we?" implored Jan Ettrich, a design manager.

"Absolutely," said project manager David Van Stan. "I would be really surprised if we don't sign a new order this week."

"Some of our guys were just in Europe," Ettrich added, "and they had some really promising leads over there."

According to Van Stan, Burger could build six yachts at a time but at that moment had just two projects under way. "If we get one more order, I think we're good," he said, sounding halfhearted at best. "That'll keep us going, don't you think?"

"Yeah, I think so," said Ettrich.

"The show feels positive," Van Stan said. "It kind of rekindles people."

MICHAEL BREMAN, Lürssen's top marketing executive, was standing not far from Burger's booth, but his perspective could not have been more different. "This is an industry that lives on wishful thinking," he said. "There's always a rainbow just around that corner over there." Lürssen had not signed a new-build contract since Lehman Brothers failed in September 2008, which was not surprising to Breman. Well before the financial crisis, he had been saying that the yacht world had become unhinged from reality.

"There was this really strange perception of the value of money," he said. "People were just paying too much for their yachts. It was as if money was worth nothing!" According to Breman, recovery would be impossible until a more rational kind of thinking returned. "We need customers who want to build boats because that's their passion. We don't want customers who build a boat just because their friend Harry has one."

Breman believed newcomers to the industry bore much of the blame for its problems. "There are about twenty shipyards around the world that can build yachts longer than forty meters," he said. "Half of those yards are an enduring part of the industry; the other half includes people who do not really understand the economics of what they are doing." He believed many of the newcomers would survive only if their owners subsidized operations with money earned from other businesses.

In the booth next to Lürssen's, Henry Luken, a television entrepreneur and yacht enthusiast, readily admitted that making money was not his foremost concern when he bought a major interest in Christensen Shipyards. The company, based in Vancouver, Washington, might be best known as the builder of Tiger Woods's 155-foot yacht *Privacy*. During the 2004 boat show, Elin Nordegren, Woods's wife at the time, visited Christensen's booth and noticed that photographs of *Privacy* were displayed together with articles about Woods, making his ownership obvious and violating a carefully crafted confidentiality agreement. Christensen later issued an apology and paid $1.6 million to Woods in damages.

"This is really a hobby for me," Luken said. "Building boats is a relationship-based business that people get into for a variety of reasons. Sometimes it's just to employ people."

Luken was not the only customer-owner at the show. At another booth, Charles Gallagher, a private investor from Denver, was chatting with several executives of Derecktor Shipyards, which had built more than two hundred yachts in Connecticut, New York, and

Florida over its sixty-year history. Derecktor had run into crippling financial difficulties while building Gallagher's 281-foot *Cakewalk,* which would become the largest yacht built on American soil since 1930, when a shipyard in Maine built the 343-foot *Corsair IV* for J.P. Morgan Jr., the legendary financier's son. Equipped with three large tenders and a wood-burning fireplace, some of *Cakewalk*'s floors would be covered with carpets that were hand-woven in Tibet on looms wide enough to eliminate the need for seams. "It is important to us to have the finest quality yacht in the world," Gallagher told one reporter. "That's what I set out for."

Like Von Allmen, Gallagher had made his fortune from buying a large number of relatively small companies. After Derecktor declared bankruptcy in the summer of 2008, he was forced to inject money into the company and fund his own yacht's construction directly. (Not long after *Cakewalk* was completed in 2010, Gallagher put it up for sale.)

KOOS ZITMAN, a senior executive at Feadship, the highly regarded Dutch yacht builder, spent his time at the show shuttling between his company's booth and its eight hundredth vessel, the 214-foot-long *Trident,* which had been dubbed the Queen of the Show. Its designer, Donald Starkey, who was helping to give tours of the yacht, estimated that it had taken more than one million man hours to produce, in large part because of its intricate interior woodwork, most of which had been fashioned from trees from Africa and Japan. Unlike at Trinity, all of the work was done by Feadship employees, which according to Zitman was a crucial competitive advantage. Opening a highly varnished closet door that had been made from "flamed mahogany," two-toned wood from the root of a very large tree, he said, "The people who do this kind of work have been with us for twenty or thirty years. If you subcontract the millwork to other companies, you don't know exactly who is going to do the work."

In business for more than one hundred years, Feadship had built ships for customers whose wealth came from a great diversity of business interests, from Henry Ford to Steve Jobs. Like Michael Breman, Zitman argued that the builders most likely to survive the crisis were those that had been around the longest. He obviously put Feadship in that category, noting that it had ten yachts under construction and had not laid off a single employee. He even suggested that economic uncertainties might be beneficial to his employer: "In a recession, customers give a lot more thought to what they're getting into. They want to know they are buying a yacht from a company that is going to be around until their boat is delivered."

Zitman had nothing but scorn for Trinity and other relatively new builders. "We have a different kind of clientele than the new builders. Our buyers are not buying a yacht because they see a 'business deal,'" an opportunity to sell a newly constructed boat for more than they paid for it. "Our customers are buying for passion." Many of the profit-seeking buyers, he predicted, would disappear along with the builders who served them. Trinity could be one of the casualties, he said, but Zitman hoped it would survive because its yachts offered a useful "reference point" to which Feadships could be favorably compared.

In truth, even Feadship was not unscathed by the financial storm. Like the Russian who commissioned *Bacarella, Trident*'s owner had not paid in full for his boat, so it too was being offered for sale. The price: $143 million. It was one of five large Feadships being marketed at the show.

14

Disaster

To the question, "When were your spirits at the lowest ebb?"
the obvious answer seemed to be "When the gin gave out."
—SIR FRANCIS CHICHESTER, WHO SINGLE-HANDEDLY SAILED
AROUND THE WORLD IN NINE MONTHS

DOUG VON Allmen made a brief visit to Trinity's hospitality center at the boat show on Thursday to talk to John Dane about the disagreement over the cost of *Lady Linda*'s woodwork. They decided to do something close to splitting the difference, with Von Allmen agreeing to pay an additional $915,000 to have Azzura execute Evan Marshall's original design. Later that day, he and Linda drove to Miami, where they spent the next two days aboard *Linda Lou*, which was docked at a marina there.

During the weekend, they received horrible news: the windfall they had expected to reap from Scott Rothstein's legal settlements was not going to happen.

When they returned to Fort Lauderdale and pulled into their driveway on Sunday, Marshall was waiting to see them. He had flown over for the show, and he wanted to talk about the location and specifications for lighting fixtures and speakers that would be installed throughout *Lady Linda*.

As they walked toward the house together, Von Allmen asked, "How's the show going?"

"Well, there are a lot of boats for sale."

Without making eye contact, Von Allmen muttered, "Oh, I bet there are!"

Marshall was carrying a roll of plans, but after he spread them across the top of the marble-topped bar where they had met many times before, he could see that Von Allmen was distracted. Staring blankly out the window, he said nothing until he stood up and left the room, saying, "I've got to get something." A minute later, Linda sat down and spoke in a quiet tone of mournfulness. "Evan, we've just heard some really terrible news. Terrible, terrible financial news." To make sure the point fully registered, she added, "We are going to put *Linda Lou* up for sale."

Marshall was perplexed. The stock market, after all, had soared in recent months, and the Von Allmens had, not long before, said they would retain *Linda Lou* and be open to the idea of making upgrades to *Lady Linda*. Alarmed by what this might mean for his project, he asked, "Do you want to slow down the project?"

"No, I don't think so, but we need to be less extravagant."

When Von Allmen returned, his wife said, "Evan just asked how we want to proceed with the new boat. Do we want to cancel it? Or put it on hold?"

"No, no," Von Allmen said. Moving his head from side to side, as if trying to shake off a bad dream, he added, "I think the best way forward is to just get it done. We're probably going to have to sell the boat, but nobody is going to buy it in its present state. What I want to do is cut back on things like bathroom fixtures and artwork. I'd like to be able to get my costs back, and people just aren't paying extra for the really extravagant stuff anymore."

SOME OF Rothstein's employees had long been skeptical about the firm's financial underpinnings. Many had the odd sense that they were being paid too much relative to the work they did. Suspicions heightened further on October 17 when Rothstein emailed them to tell them about a "client" who was facing a variety of criminal charges—fraud, money laundering, and embezzlement—and wanted to flee to a country from which he could not be extradited. "Time is of the essence," Rothstein wrote. "Let's rock and roll . . . There is a very large fee attached to this case. Thanks. Love ya Scott."

The Von Allmens had also become suspicious. A large payment that was supposed to have been sent to them had not arrived. On Monday, October 26—three days before the start of the boat show— Linda walked into Bova Prime, Rothstein's restaurant, and spotted him drinking a martini at the bar. When she confronted him, he refused to answer her questions. "Sorry, I'm having a bad day," he said before turning away.

It would soon become apparent that virtually all of the money that was supposed to have been in the "locked accounts," as well as funds belonging to Rothstein's law firm and its clients, had disappeared. It was (and would remain) unclear where most of the money went (or, for that matter, exactly how much there had been), but $16 million was wired to a bank account Rothstein had recently opened in Morocco, a country his colleagues had identified as not having an extradition treaty with the United States. On Tuesday night, October 27, Rothstein boarded a large private plane, a Gulfstream V, which took him there.

Not everything Rothstein had told Von Allmen was a complete lie. His law firm actually did represent an alleged victim of Jeffrey Epstein's in a pending civil suit—Rothstein had shown Von Allmen documents from that case—but Rothstein's claims that he represented multiple victims and had discovered evidence of improprieties, on Epstein's plane or anywhere else, and that he had negotiated settlements were untrue. Other elements of Rothstein's story were entirely fictitious. Rothstein did not represent plaintiffs in any litigation against Chiquita, and the alleged settlements with the company were fabricated. The bank statements Von Allmen had seen were all bogus. It also turned out that Michael Szafranski, who Von Allmen paid to serve as the "confirming agent," was also receiving money from Rothstein: almost $6.5 million since July. Later on, during proceedings relating to the bankruptcy of Rothstein's business, when Szafranski was asked about his role, he repeatedly invoked his Fifth Amendment right to avoid self-incrimination; he eventually agreed to a settlement that required him to pay more than $6 million to the bankruptcy trustee.

In classic Ponzi scheme fashion, the profits Rothstein had promised to his investors could come only from new ones, and even with Von Allmen's infusions, there was not nearly enough money to keep the ball rolling.

On October 31 Rothstein sent a text message from Morocco to his law partners that read like a suicide note: "Sorry for letting you all down. I am a fool. I thought I could fix it, but got trapped by my ego and refusal to fail, and now all I have accomplished is hurting people I love. Please take care of yourselves and please protect Kimmie. She knew nothing. Neither did she, nor any of you, deserve what I did. I hope God allows me to see you on the other side. Love, Scott."

After Von Allmen learned that none of the legal settlements he had purchased was real, he found it difficult to sleep at night. He had lost such a substantial portion of his wealth that he made plans to send *Linda Lou* to the Persian Gulf, where he hoped it could be sold to an oil-rich Arab. And once again, he altered his approach for building *Lady Linda,* starting with the lighting fixtures that Marshall had wanted to discuss. Von Allmen had been thinking about using LED lights for overhead fixtures, but not anymore. They would create less heat and use less energy, but they would require $60,000 in extra costs—and Von Allmen, suddenly afraid that he could not afford even one yacht, no longer thought of himself as *Lady Linda*'s long-term owner.

15

I'd Rather Be Surfing

Fortune brings in some boats that are not steered.

—*Cymbeline*, William Shakespeare

DURING THE last week of March 2010, what would become the front of a bedside table in one of *Lady Linda*'s guest staterooms was lying on a workbench several hundred miles north of Sydney, Australia. In the early morning light, it didn't look like much, just a square piece of plywood. But by the end of the day, Mitch Davies, a New Zealander who, not many years earlier, had ranked as his country's best eighteen-and-under surfer, would endow the panel with a very different appearance.

Like all of the cabinetry, the bedside table had been designed by Evan Marshall. The panel Davies was working on would be sheathed with an intricate pattern of wood veneers, most of them from burl wood. He had started his workday by going to a storeroom to find several sheets of veneer that had been cut from a burled section of a beech tree. The rippled one-foot-by-one-foot sheets were less than a millimeter thick—not much more than paper—and they were dry and rough; so brittle that it seemed like any handling would cause them to crumble like a potato chip. Once Davies laid them out on a large worktable, the most prominent features were tightly bunched swirls of black dots that looked like tiny knotholes.

His first task was to choose four eight-by-seven-inch sections of veneer. There were two criteria for their selection. First, the rectangles had to be visually interesting; Davies judged areas with no obvious signs of burl to be boring. Second, each pair needed to be book-matched, so that their grain patterns would appear to be mirror images of each other. The sheets had been cut sequentially from the same tree, so one sheet was quite similar to the next, but there were always slight variations. Davies regarded this as a plus, saying, "It's the beauty of working with a natural product." This part of his job was as much about design as it was woodworking, which also appealed to him. It was also one of the reasons that at least two-thirds of the veneer would end up unused.

Once he had picked the two sections, Davies placed a heavy straight-edge along the borders and further confirmed his selection by using

Mitch Davies selects bookmarked sections of burl wood.

his forearm to hold the metal in place. Then he slid the scalpel along the edge of the metal. The movement was steady and smooth, and the blade was sharp, but because he could not apply much pressure against the delicate material, he had to repeat the motion four times before the separation was complete. Everything about his work required absolute precision, along with a kind of patience not always found among young men. For Davies, these were tasks from which he derived tremendous satisfaction and pride—and he said that was the most important factor in doing his work well.

★

DAVIES HAD always been happy with his place in the world. His childhood home was next to a black-sand beach on New Zealand's north island and within sight of mountains. He started surfing, skiing, and skateboarding when he was very young, and he became good enough to pursue all three competitively. "If the sun was shining, we were outside playing," he remembered. "If it was raining, we were still outside playing. It was a pretty bliss life." The only thing that did not suit him was school. He enjoyed two of his classes—woodshop and mechanical drawing—but nothing else held his interest. When his teachers refused to give him time off to train for a surfing competition in Australia during his senior year in high school, he dropped out. Now twenty-five, he had no regrets. "I'm very happy I didn't go back," he said. "It wasn't me."

Like almost everyone in New Zealand, where 90 percent of the population lives close to the sea, Davies also grew up with boats. His father helped him build a dinghy when he was twelve. As a teenager, he carved miniature versions of sailboat hulls. "I just loved taking a piece of wood and trying to turn it into something," he said. The models also gave him the idea that he could make a living from constructing full-sized boats. His father was a home builder, and Davies helped with several projects, but boats held greater appeal. "Houses are rougher," Davies explained. "You walk into a room, there's a door and a window and some furniture. On a boat, there's more detail, and almost everything is wood. Everything has to be much more precise, which means you always have to do the best work that you can." He applied for cabinetmaking apprenticeships with several shipbuilders, and Alloy Yachts, New Zealand's biggest custom-yacht builder, offered him a position. By the time he completed the four-year program in early 2008, he had accumulated eight thousand hours of experience.

With the yacht-building industry operating at full tilt, Davies knew finding a job would not be difficult. The demand for cabinet-makers was particularly fierce, and Davies was recruited and hired by a shipyard in Southampton, England. He was paid extremely well: the equivalent of $55 New Zealand dollars per hour (US $38 at the time), and the company also covered the costs of his accommodations and food. He relocated to Australia in February after a childhood friend told him that Azzura Marine was hiring dozens of craftsmen to create *Lady Linda*'s interior. As much as anything, Davies agreed to go because of Azzura's location near Australia's Gold Coast, the legendary stretch of ocean beach where he had gone for the surfing competition that caused him to leave school. In spite of his youth, his starting hourly wage was $24, more than what Gale Tribble was paid after forty years of work.

Handsome and bright eyed, Davies does not look anything like Tribble—Brad Pitt offers a closer comparison—but both men shared the early-morning regimen of blue-collar workers everywhere. Davies lived in a small two-bedroom duplex apartment about twenty miles from the factory with his long-term girlfriend and another young couple. The layout was basic: two small bedrooms and a bathroom upstairs and an open space on the ground floor that functioned as a living room and kitchen. The low-rise building was an out-of-date oddity in a neighborhood dominated by gleaming high-rise condominiums, most of them occupied by vacationers and retirees.

Davies's schedule was also totally out of sync with those of most of his neighbors and his apartment mates, who all worked at restaurants. That meant he never had to worry about getting into the apartment's one bathroom when his alarm clock sounded at 4:55 a.m. His morning routine was swiftly accomplished. He laid out his work clothes—a T-shirt, a pair of shorts that extended below his knees, sneakers, and socks—the night before. As soon as he was dressed, he went downstairs to remove three premade sandwiches from the refrigerator. The fridge was organized carefully, with designated shelves for each couple, but the rest of the apartment was youthful mayhem. An extraordinarily lumpy couch was covered with a red blanket. The cinder-block walls were lined with cardboard boxes, and bicycles leaned against the boxes. While Davies spent his days turning exotic woods into fine furniture, nothing in this room was made from natural timber. The apartment did have two important attributes: it was inexpensive—he and his girlfriend paid less than $200 a month for their half of the rent—and it was just one block from the beach.

On the day he assembled the front panel of one of *Lady Linda*'s bedside tables, Davies stepped outside at 5:15 a.m. As he walked to his car, the condominium towers appeared as gloomy silhouettes against the still-dark sky. The car, a much-dented station wagon, had an odd quirk: the radio was always on, locked to a single station and an unchangeable volume level. With almost no other cars on the road, the drive was also uncomplicated. When Davies found a parking space a few minutes before the six o'clock start of the workday, the sun still hadn't risen, but the edges of the sky were brightening with orange.

The work environment was very different from Trinity's. Employees were required to slide identification cards through a time clock, but there were no guards or security gate, and the building was clean and brightly lit. After daybreak, natural light would enter through enormous bays that were left open to the outside during most of the year. Large spotlights hung from the ceiling, and fluorescent fixtures were positioned above single-person work stations, which were widely separated from one another. The concrete floors were clean, and so was the bathroom. And unlike at Trinity, where workers sat on toolboxes and picnic tables on the production floor during breaks and lunch, Azzura had a dedicated lunchroom, which was decorated with photographs of previous Azzura projects. Just outside the lunchroom were a patio and a grill, which were put to use during twice-a-month Friday afternoon barbeques.

Azzura's thirty-one craftsmen were all working on *Lady Linda*. Most of them were new employees, recruited after Azzura was awarded the contract for the yacht's interior. Because the rest of the vessel was being built thousands of miles away, there was an odd sense of remove, although, in some ways, Azzura's employees had a closer connection to the final product than Trinity's. Evan Marshall's renderings were posted on the walls, and, unlike most of the laborers who were involved in the project, Azzura's were creating things the Von Allmens would see and touch. And while workers in Gulfport had never heard the owner's name—they always referred to the project as T-50, Trinity's official name—at Azzura it was always called *Lady Linda* or "the Von Allmens' yacht."

ONCE DAVIES had cut the four rectangles of beech burl veneer he wanted, he glued them to the plywood panel. He did this very carefully, one drop at a time. If he used too little, the veneer would bubble; if he used too much, it would end up spreading onto the front surface and mar its appearance. Later the rectangles would be stained brown and surrounded by a thin border created by a different veneer, lacewood, a light-toned wood with tightly interwoven grain lines that gave it a snakeskin-like appearance.

Davies approved of the design. "What I really like are the contrasts between the dark and light woods," he said. However, those contrasts made the job of gluing the veneers to the panel all the more challenging. If the margins were inconsistent, the imperfections would be all the more obvious. "If you're off by a millimeter," Davies explained, "people will focus on what's wrong with the furniture instead of what's great about it."

In every aspect, the pace of veneer work was slow—so slow it sometimes looked like Davies was losing time to indecision and procrastination. "People don't understand how it can take so long to build things with this kind of quality," he said, "but that's just the way it is."

Everything Azzura did swallowed up extraordinary amounts of time. A few steps away from Davies, Grant Houston, a fifty-one-year-old Australian, was assembling a closet door for one of the guest staterooms that would have ten layers. The outermost surfaces would be made from several different wood veneers, while the interior would include two layers of balsa wood, another two of Formica, and four different sections of fiberglass. Designed so that it would not warp and would be fire resistant, it would take thirty hours of labor to assemble the pieces and another ten for sanding and varnishing. "The time just runs away from you on these boats," Houston said.

Four hours after Davies started work on the front of the bedside table, he had glued all of the veneers to the plywood panel, which he placed inside a heat press that would help to join the materials permanently. A rather dramatic step remained: because the cabinet would have drawers and the panel would become the drawer fronts, it would be sliced into three pieces. But when Davies removed the panel from the heat press, he seemed pleased by his handiwork thus far, saying, "I'm sure the Von Allmens will be very happy when they see this." Then he had second thoughts. He was beginning to think he did not like the outside corners of each of the sections of beech burl. The constellation of burl marks in the corners nearest to the center of the panel was interesting enough, but there wasn't much going on near the outside corners. "It's not bad," he said, "but it could be better."

NOT FAR away, Travis Brown was working on the rest of the bedside table. When it was completed, it would be a piece of furniture that would function no differently from something that could be purchased at a retail store for a couple of hundred dollars, but *Lady Linda*'s version was a complicated construction. In contrast to production-line-manufactured furniture, for which the number of materials and components is minimized, this would contain four different species of wood and dozens of pieces. Except for the veneering and the varnishing, Brown would build the cabinet without help from anyone else. He had been at it for two weeks and expected to be done in another day or two.

Intensely focused, Brown wore headphones during most of the day. It looked like he was listening to music, but he wasn't; the device's only purpose was to block out sound. A fellow New Zealander, Brown had gone to school with Davies and was the friend who had told him about Azzura.

Brown's first job out of school was in a concrete plant. He later came to the conclusion that jobs requiring greater levels of precision were more rewarding, both in satisfaction and financially. He tried plumbing before he started working with wood, which he liked much more. "There is meaning in this work," he said. "A ton of work goes into each piece of furniture, and it shows." Now twenty-four, he enjoyed his work so much that he spent much of his free time doing the same thing. In his home workshop, he was trying to carve a log into what would look like interlocking links of chain.

A couple of days later, after the bedside table was fully assembled, Brown carried it to the full-scale mockup of *Lady Linda*'s lower deck that had been constructed to confirm that everything Azzura made would fit. From the outside, the mockup looked like an enormous cardboard box. The inside was divided into compartments, and the floors were marked to indicate the locations of beds, closets, cabinets, vanities, and doors. Other lines showed the position of each of the frames that Gale Tribble had joined almost two years earlier. The representations of the structural elements were all labeled and numbered, and the crisscrossing lines could be used to identify locations like the latitudes and longitudes of a geographic map. *Lady Linda*'s floors would be marked in exactly the same way.

The bedside table would be connected to a wall and a bed, and it would be obvious if any of its dimensions was off because Marshall had designed a base molding that would carry over from the wall to the bedside table and then to the bed. The molding was to be made with a layer cake of wood: verbena burl and lacewood veneers, which would be separated by a strip of mahogany that protruded from the surface of the other woods. If the bands of wood on the wall did not meet up with the corresponding sections on the table and the bed, the discrepancies would be impossible to miss.

After the dimensions of the furniture and paneling were confirmed as perfect, the bedside table would be taken to the finishing shop. There it would be partially disassembled so varnish would not accumulate in joints and corners. The finishing process would take place in several repetitive steps: sanding, a spray-gun application of varnish, followed by more sanding and more varnishing as well as buffing and polishing until the desired level of gloss was achieved. According to Marshall's specifications, most of *Lady Linda*'s woodwork needed to have a mirrorlike reflective shine. Depending on the type of wood, achieving that would require five to nine coats of varnish.

Once the finishing work was done, each piece of furniture would be reassembled to ensure that everything still fit together tightly. Then the final product would be covered in protective wrapping and packed into containers that would be sent by ship to Gulfport.

RICHARD MEESTER was inside the mockup, standing on a ladder in the corner of one of the guest staterooms. He had already braced a rounded length of a light-toned wood, rock maple, which would serve as the crown molding, to one of the walls. Now he was working on a different section, which would go on the adjacent wall. The molding was large and heavy—four inches thick, it extended eight inches out from the wall—but it would not be attached to the ceiling. Instead, the uppermost surface would hang two inches below to create a recess between it and the ceiling that would conceal air-conditioning vents and lights.

If the molding was going to be painted, the gaps of a less than perfect joint could be overcome readily with wood filler and paint, and Meester could erect four walls of molding in just a few hours. But this molding would not be painted. Like the furniture, it would have a "real wood" finish, so each section had to fit into the next one perfectly. "Most people assume it's just a matter of cutting two lengths of wood at forty-five-degree angles and putting them together," said Meester. "But it never works out that way. Timber isn't perfectly straight, and the saw isn't absolutely accurate. It usually takes four or five cuts" by a table saw and then plenty of sanding to achieve a satisfactory fit. As with the base molding, a detail of Marshall's design—the surface of the molding farthest from the wall was rounded, and there was a protrusion from the center that Meester called a "nipple"—made precision all the more critical. Meester estimated that it would take two full weeks to complete molding in each of the four guest staterooms.

Woodworking was a second career for Meester, a balding forty-two-year-old. His first was affiliated—he had been a salesman for a timber importer in his native Holland—but altogether different. He hated the paperwork and being tied to a desk; he wanted to actually make things. Too old for a formal apprenticeship, Meester found a furniture maker who was willing to give him on-the-job training. He moved to Australia with his wife and two young children after hearing about Azzura's contract to build *Lady Linda*'s interior.

Meester had already cut the end of the second piece of molding two times and was recalibrating the angle of the saw's circular blade for a third cut when an additional complication arose. A supervisor, Damien Thomas, announced that components of the king-sized bed that had been made for the compartment in which Meester was working would be assembled there. Although he didn't say so to Thomas, Meester was appalled. Bringing the bed into the relatively small space would slow down everything, and the bed could easily be damaged. "It doesn't make any sense," he whispered. But Thomas had other priorities. Since the bed, which had taken four weeks to assemble, was the prototype for those in the other guest staterooms, he was eager to confirm its specifications so construction on the others could commence. He also wanted to send the first bed to the finishing shop to prevent that part of the process from becoming a bottleneck to the overall production effort.

In the larger scheme of things, Meester's frustration was minor, but it illustrated an essential truth: at various times, every worker, every department, and every company involved in building *Lady Linda* believed its job was not just important but *more important* than everyone else's. Regardless of whether or not they were right, priorities came into conflict.

Meester would end up running the second section of the crown molding back through the table saw five times, and his work was, in fact, delayed by the bed. Even when the joint was close to perfect, some sections had to be shaped further with sandpaper.

AZZURA'S THREE-PERSON executive team and four production designers worked from a single room up a set of stairs from the production floor. The designers were responsible for turning Marshall's three-dimensional conceptual plans into detailed schematic drawings. Those translations used to be made by cabinetmakers, but computers can do the work more efficiently, and they can also turn out precise specifications that can be fed to the machines that cut lumber into the desired sizes and shapes.

While Meester was working on the crown molding, the designers were focused on the next phase of construction: the compartment on the sky lounge level that would be used as both a bedroom and a gym. The dual purposes had led to a problem: the Von Allmens wanted it to be equipped with a treadmill that could be removed when it was not being used, but the room's closet would not be large enough to hold the machine. "Trinity says that's okay because they say it can be folded up and carried in and out of the room and taken somewhere else," said Craig Rothwell, the Azzura manager who managed the design team and who had already been to Gulfport, "but we're not sure there's a treadmill that's small enough to go through the door." And even if there was, he did not like the idea of asking the crew to carry a heavy piece of equipment through a narrow space and past a door that had taken forty hours to construct.

At 4:00 p.m., a horn signaled the official end of the day. Employees were encouraged to put in another hour, but it was optional, and Davies, eager always to go surfing, never did. By 4:40, he had been to his apartment and was striding toward the beach. Since his arrival in Australia two months earlier, he had surfed every day except for six. This would become the seventh. The ocean was so calm that he ended up at the Kurrawa Surf Club, where he sat down on a deck overlooking the beach and ordered a beer. The first thing he talked about was surfing's appeal: "To start with, you're on the water, and for me, that's peace and comfort. At the same time, there's a challenge: no two waves are the same. You can catch a hundred of them, and every one is going to be different." When he was competing, Davies was known for the relaxed, almost fluid way in which he moved his body over the board. "I'm not as good as I used to be, so it's more for pure enjoyment now," he said. "But I still push myself. And when the surf gets up, my heart gets pumping."

While Von Allmen's unhappiness with factory work had spurred life-changing ambition, that seemed unlikely for Davies. In his childhood neighborhood, most people worked as farmers or in the oil industry. The wealthiest person he knew was a professional scuba diver who spent most of his time working on offshore oil rigs. Davies's work on yachts had left him with a much more expansive understanding of the rewards that could come from more substantial wealth, but he wasn't interested. "I'm glad Doug Von Allmen is rich," he said. "If it wasn't for rich people, I wouldn't have my job. But it's not a goal of mine. I don't think it's worth the stress. And I think that if you want to be rich, you never have enough. I don't want that. I just want to have a happy life and be myself."

Davies's financial life was as uncomplicated as his way of thinking. Other than the apartment rent, his only obligation was the mortgage on a house he had recently bought in his hometown back in New Zealand. It wasn't on the beach like his parents' home, but it was just a few blocks away. With a down payment he had saved from working in England, he paid $180,000 for the three-bedroom house. The monthly mortgage payment was manageable, less than $150. There was another somewhat pressing financial matter—saving enough money to buy an engagement ring for his girlfriend—but his long-term goal of raising children in the same small community where he grew up was already within reach.

Davies was home by seven thirty. He usually went to bed by eight thirty, never after nine thirty. Even on weekends, he did not like to stay up much later. "It ruins my sleep pattern," he explained.

AT SOME point, everyone who has anything to do with megayachts trades stories about the most extravagant extremes of their creations. David McQueen, Azzura's chief executive, said his favorite was a yacht that had a compartment that looked like a movie theater but had just two seats; its sole purpose was to provide an onboard runway on which fashion house models could strut their latest offerings. But McQueen, an Englishman who got his start in the business as an apprentice cabinetmaker on the Isle of Wight, was quick to add that the excesses of some created jobs for many others. And the larger the extravagance, the greater the number of jobs. Given that wages account for two-thirds of a yacht's cost, he said, "You could say that *all* these giant boats are a total waste of money, but that money pays a lot of mortgages. It gives the people who work here freedom to live their lives."

Still, he could not help but wish that yacht owners did things differently sometimes. Picking up one of more than forty wood samples that would soon be sent to Von Allmen to show him what the final finishes would look like, he noted that all of the wood in *Lady Linda*'s interior would be stained before it was varnished, making it impossible to see the natural color of the woods. He also thought the finishes were too glossy. "We're using all of this beautiful wood, but then we're covering it up," he said. There will be so much varnish that it might end up being thicker than the veneer. "It gets to a point that it isn't really wood anymore—it looks like plastic."

16

Sell Everything

The sea's in my veins, my tradition remains, I'm just glad I don't live in a trailer.

—"Son of a Son of a Sailor," Jimmy Buffett

It was May 2010, and Doug Von Allmen was seated in his seventy-fourth-floor living room in Manhattan, where he had discussed *Lady Linda*'s design with Evan Marshall two and a half years earlier. But the circumstances were now quite different: he was talking not about boat building but about how he had lost more than $100 million to Scott Rothstein's Ponzi scheme—and whether he could afford to be *Lady Linda*'s owner.

Von Allmen's initial reaction to the bad news had been a mix of emotional distress and denial. When he spoke to Bob Norman, the journalist who followed the story more closely than anyone else, shortly after Rothstein was exposed, he downplayed the impact of the loss: "It won't change my lifestyle that much, but it was a nice sum. I will still eat out at a restaurant every night. This is just something I need to get through."

Now, several months later, Von Allmen admitted that the missing money would have a profound impact. The evidence of this started with the apartment itself, which he was trying to sell. The asking price was $18.45 million, and he expected to finalize the sale, to a Russian, for about $3 million less than that, within a few days. He was also trying to sell most of the apartment's contents. Furniture, paintings, knickknacks—even garbage pails—were all labeled with detailed descriptions and prices. Although nothing was inexpensive, the little signs had transformed the grand apartment into a kind of rarified tag sale. The label taped to the round table where he had sat with Marshall during the design meeting and later with John Dane when he told him he was returning the 157-footer to Trinity indicated that it was covered with lacquered parchment and could be purchased for $10,500.

With so many wealthy residents, many of them older, South Florida had seen more than its share of financial fraud, but never a scam as large as Rothstein's. On some level, it was impossible not to be impressed by his diabolical creativity: the extraordinary fabrications and his ability to combine them with a semilegitimate law firm and checkbook-acquired political relationships to fool sophisticated investors into believing they were fortunate to be included. The supposed need for confidentiality had been a crucial ingredient, providing not only a ready means for obscuring the facts but also logic for the notion that Rothstein accepted money only from people he knew. So too was the extravagant spending, which had helped to make the dream look real.

No one had lost more money than Von Allmen, and as Florida newspapers sought to make sense of the story, his personal reputation became an additional casualty. Norman posted almost daily stories on his paper's website, and a few readers posted comments that claimed Von Allmen had played an active role in perpetuating the scheme. "Doug wants everyone to believe that he and his family are victims of the Ponzi," wrote one. This reader then went on to level an accusation and a warning: "Doug was one of the 'feeders' of the Ponzi scheme to recapture his lost investments. Doug truly is one of the 'Devils' behind the scenes . . . Maybe Linda should try cooking some meals for the table to try to bring them back down to earth. In any event, stay tuned and keep your eyes on Doug Von Allmen. He's the guy. Look out Doug. They're on to you now."

Sitting in his living room, Von Allmen said he had encouraged only family members and one friend to invest and that he did not know Rothstein was a fraud until shortly before he fled the country. He was not embarrassed about his own participation, his initial stress and denial having been displaced by clear-headed stoicism. "I have nobody to blame for this but myself," he said. "I was blinded by the returns." He also cited two other factors. First, his mistaken belief that Rothstein had been pedaling his legal settlements for seven years, when it had actually been just four: "I thought it had been going for a long time and that it would have collapsed by then if it was a Ponzi scheme." The TD Bank account statements he had been shown were the other factor: "I thought the only way it could be a fraud was if the bank was in on it—and I thought there was no way the bank could have been in on it."

Von Allmen said he had some understanding of what drove Rothstein to cheat. "I've seen how people get into a lifestyle," he said. "And after a while, they think that if they don't look successful that they can't be successful." At the same time, though, he was mystified by Rothstein's goal and his endgame. Rothstein, after all, must have understood that sooner or later every Ponzi scheme is exposed, and he must have realized that he had grown his so rapidly that it could not be sustained nearly so long as, say, Bernie Madoff's decades-long swindle. Unable to come up with a plausible explanation, Von Allmen wondered if drugs or a psychological disorder played a role.

Shortly after the scheme was discovered, he hired William Scherer, a highly regarded litigator, who had been gathering facts for a lawsuit. "It is unbelievably complicated," Von Allmen said. Even the amount of money lost by investors was difficult to determine. While press reports put it at somewhere greater than $1 billion, Von Allmen said it was much less than that because some of the supposed losses appeared to be fictitious. Von Allmen estimated the total amount of money lost at "something like five hundred million." The question of where it went was also complicated. It appeared that Rothstein himself had swallowed up about $160 million—money spent on houses, cars, jewelry, and his boat as well as propping up his law firm and acquiring interests in several restaurants and other businesses. Of the balance, a very large portion, about $300 million, disappeared during the three months prior to the scheme's downfall.

Rothstein had returned from Morocco in early November. Pleading guilty to money laundering and several other felonies, he was sent to prison for fifty years. Most of his personal assets were sold, yielding millions of dollars that would be used to reimburse investors for their losses, but it was not nearly enough. The 1,329-page suit filed by Scherer named several other defendants that were much better capitalized than Rothstein: TD Bank, Rothstein's accounting firm, an "investor" who had allegedly conspired with Rothstein, and a hedge fund that was accused of discovering the fraud and demanding its money back in return for its silence, potentially giving it the liability of a coconspirator. The accountants were guilty of "unforgivable errors," the suit charged, because they gave their "seal of approval to a Ponzi scheme premised upon phantom investments, paying phantom plaintiffs, and authenticating phantom receivables."

Fortunately for Von Allmen, the case would be tried before a jury under Florida law, which enabled him to claim treble damages. Scherer believed TD Bank and some of the other defendants would eventually agree to settlements with Von Allmen and other victims that would at least cover their losses and legal fees in order to avoid additional adverse publicity and the risk of even greater damages. "Juries don't like rich people, but they dislike banks even more," Von Allmen said. "Scherer tells me that at a minimum I will get my money back and the legal fees. It's up to me whether I want to press for more."

After talking about Rothstein for a couple of hours from his chair in the living room, Von Allmen went upstairs to his office to look for some financial records he could access only through his desktop computer. Linda was also on that floor, showing a pair of auction house appraisers some furniture. Sitting down at a desk from which he had the same panoramic view as downstairs, Von Allmen admitted to being annoyed that after so many years of success, he had to ratchet back his lifestyle now, a year before his seventieth birthday. At the same time, though, he had already accepted the reality that endless improvements to his wealth and lifestyle were a thing of the past.

He even suggested that might not be all bad. "There are going to be some things I can't have and things that I can't do," he said. "But you know . . . I have been poor and I've been what I guess you could call rich"—the son of a milkman was still not entirely comfortable using that word to describe himself—"and to tell you the truth, it's easier to be poor than it is to be rich." Gesturing toward the hall where a housekeeper had just started vacuuming, he said, "When you're poor, you don't need to have all these people around you all the time."

Von Allmen went on to admit that his finances would be strained even after the apartment was sold. A favorable settlement to his lawsuit would change that, but the likelihood of that was uncertain and so too was the timing. His biggest problems were the cost of completing *Lady Linda* and the more than $5 million he spent every year to maintain *Linda Lou*. He had already put the bigger boat on the market. Now he admitted that the ultimate consequence could be even worse: even if he found a buyer for that yacht, he might have to also sell *Lady Linda,* perhaps before it was completed.

17

Another Fall

The sea is the same as it has been since before men ever went on it in boats.

—ERNEST HEMINGWAY

DURING THE spring of 2010, Gale Tribble was also having a tough time. Almost every day, starting a couple of hours after he woke up, pulsating pain stabbed at the top of his head. Assuming too much beer was to blame, he reduced his consumption to just one or two twelve-ounce cans a day, but that did not make any difference. Aspirin did not help either. A different pain reliever, Goody's Extra Strength Headache Powders, was somewhat more effective, but only briefly. And on mornings when he woke up with a headache, which happened about once a week, he knew the pain would remain no matter what he did.

Tribble was also having trouble with his legs. Like the head-aches, the problems typically commenced during the morning, usu-ally with a tingling sensation below his knees, followed by throbbing pain. Sometimes one or both legs went numb, which led him to worry that he would fall. The only way he could regain normal sen-sation was to shake his feet and pound them on the floor. Aches and pains were not new to Tribble. He had been troubled by backaches for many years. They seemed to develop whenever his work required him to hold his arms above his head for prolonged periods of time. But he knew the new afflictions were more serious, and additional health issues emerged throughout the spring and summer. Some days his feet, particularly his left one, became swollen. And when he stood up, he sometimes felt disoriented and unstable, as if he were going to faint.

Tribble had always been reluctant to call a doctor, but he was sufficiently concerned that he eventually did see his physician, who said his blood pressure was far too high and gave him a prescription. Almost immediately, the headaches diminished. The dizzy spells also became less severe, though he still felt light-headed whenever he rose after a long stretch of working on his knees. His leg problems were entirely unaffected by the medication. Attributing the problem to bad circulation, the doctor suggested that it was something that could not be cured.

On the Friday before Memorial Day weekend, Tribble did take a fall, from a ladder. He was aboard *Cocoa Bean,* the 242-foot yacht, and he was in a hurry. There were dozens of people working on the vast vessel, and many of them wanted to use the main stair-case to move between the decks, but it had been blocked off by a sheet of metal that extended across part of the stairwell. Tribble was using an electric grinder to cut it away. He had been making steady progress until just after eleven in the morning when the extension cord, which went to an outlet on the upper deck, disconnected. To plug it in again, Tribble climbed a steeply pitched ladder that passed through an opening to the deck above. His legs were not bother-ing him much that day, but he was trying to move quickly, and that may explain why he missed the top step when he started back down the ladder. Falling about eight feet, he knew his left foot, the one that had been bothering him the most, absorbed the worst of the impact, but he was unclear about the exact details of what hap-pened next. When Brian Brenner, another shipfitter, found him sprawled on the deck, Tribble's elbow was bleeding, his left leg was wracked with pain, his head hurt, and his helmet was nowhere to be seen.

"What the hell—are you all right?" Brenner asked as he helped Tribble to sit up.

"Man, I don't know," Tribble replied.

Tribble was in a daze. He thought he had lost consciousness, so he was not sure how long he had been on the floor. Brenner helped him to hobble slowly off the vessel to the "safety office," a small room in a cinder-block structure near the center of the production floor. A sign just outside the door read: "The company has worked for 63 days without a lost-time accident. The best previous record was 165 days. Do your part. Help us make a new record."

Paul Gustafson, the safety officer, told Tribble to sit in a decrepit one-time barber's chair in the center of the room.

"Are you hurting?" he asked.

Thinking the answer should be obvious, Tribble was annoyed by the question. "Hell yes!" he said.

"*Where* are you hurting?"

"I'm hurting all over!"

"Why don't you take off your shoes and try to move your toes and fingers," Gustafson suggested. Once he saw movements, he said, "Nothing is broken."

This made Tribble even more angry. "Where did you get your medical degree?" he said sarcastically to himself. He was further aggravated when Gustafson didn't have any ice or ACE bandages. Giving Tribble two aspirin tablets, the safety officer told him to buy some bandages on the way home. "Why don't you take it easy over the weekend and see how you feel next week?" he suggested. Tribble thought he should see a doctor, but he returned to where he had been working and did not go home until the end-of-work siren sounded at two thirty. He spent most of the long weekend sitting on his favorite blue-and-green chair, watching television.

At six o'clock on Tuesday morning, Tribble returned to the safety office and told Gustafson that his foot, arm, and back still hurt.

"What did you do over the weekend?" he asked.

"Not a damn thing!"

"Well, that's probably why you're sore. What you need is some exercise. Why don't you go out and do some work and see how you're feeling after that?"

Tribble, who had been injured on the job only once before, still thought he should see a doctor. But he didn't argue and he didn't miss any days—or even hours—of work because of the accident, so the safety office's no-lost-time clock continued to advance. But he felt like he had been mistreated; that his relationship with Trinity had changed. Until then he had felt a great sense of loyalty to the company, and he had thought it was mutual.

During the weeks that followed, his bitterness only deepened whenever he saw Gustafson walking around the yard. He spent much of his time talking to workers and reminding them to put on their helmets and safety masks, but he never stopped to ask Tribble about his injuries. He suspected that Gustafson was motivated by more selfish concerns. Every two months, Trinity's laborers were eligible for a $175 performance bonus for which there were three requirements: workers could miss no more than one day of work, not leave early more than twice, and not be cited for any safety rule violations. Tribble knew that management employees also received bonuses, and he wondered whether Gustafson's was based partly on the no-lost-time numbers.

Tribble's other challenge was the summer heat, which seemed to aggravate the problems with his legs. Sometimes they were so unresponsive that they felt as if they were no longer connected to the rest of his body. He told his supervisor he could not climb ladders anymore, but even stairs were a concern. Getting his feet from one step to another required total concentration, and sometimes that was insufficient, so he had to grab the back of each thigh and pull the leg upward, one at a time. His back pains were also worsening. Whenever he held up his arms to grind or weld, even for short periods, his shoulders and upper back felt like they were burning. "The mornings usually aren't so bad," he said in late June, "but after lunch, it gets to the point where I say to myself, 'I've just got to go home.'"

Tribble celebrated his sixty-second birthday on June 14, and he knew his afflictions would only worsen. He had been crouching, crawling, and kneeling in cramped spaces and on hard surfaces for forty-three years. Few shipyard laborers lasted much longer than that. But while his job had resulted in probably irreversible damage to his health and body, he was not outraged in the way people in other lines of work might imagine. Tribble saw it as the normal course of things. "When you have a job like mine and you get to be my age, this is what happens," he said. "Stuff deteriorates."

LIKE TRIBBLE, Trinity was also struggling. During the first half of 2010, it laid off 20 percent of its employees and scaled back the standard workweek from forty-eight hours to forty for almost all of the survivors, Tribble among them. John Dane was spending much of his time trying to drum up nonyacht projects, and he had found some success, winning contracts to build several high-speed naval patrol boats for Kuwait and a pair of large oceangoing tugboats.

In July Tribble started working on the hull of one of the tugs, and his forty-eight-hour schedule was restored. He could not decide whether he should be pleased or not. He was happy to have the larger paycheck, but getting through the day was tougher than ever, and he didn't like working on the tugs. Their hulls were being made not from aluminum but steel, which is much heavier, so the components were difficult to move. Unpainted and rusting, they left his clothes with a constant layer of red-black grit. "You feel like you've been wallowing in dirt all day," he said.

Tribble was also unhappy with changes in the way the yard was managed. In early August he was told he should no longer go to the toolroom when he needed something. Instead, a large metal box containing various kinds of equipment was placed close to the tug. However, since the box was generally locked, he had to wait for a foreman to provide access. "When a lightbulb blows, I used to go the toolroom and get a new one," Tribble said. "It took ten minutes. Now I have to go to the box and wait for someone to unlock it. That can take an hour." Tribble was also told that he must use the bathroom and water cooler that were closest to the tug and that he could not go to the bathroom during the twenty minutes just before and after the lunch break. The rules had obviously been instituted in the name of efficiency. Some workers used to make a habit of walking to distant water fountains. Some disliked their jobs so much that they hid out in the graffiti-covered stalls of the foul-smelling bathrooms. Others went to a bathroom near the parking lot just before lunch so they could beat the line at Sugar Mamas, the food-vending van.

To an extent, Tribble said he understood management's position—"some people act like tourists and walk around a lot," he acknowledged—but he was nonetheless offended by the changed approach and the implication that he could not be trusted. That bothered him more than the realization that his health had been impaired by his work. The physical damage was inevitable. The lack of respect was a choice. "I don't know about you, but I can't control when I need to go to the bathroom," he said. "Believe it or not, they've been having people monitor the bathrooms! It's crazy. I don't go to the toilet and sit there! I go and get out as quick as possible. It doesn't smell very inviting in there. I don't know what's gotten into this place."

THROUGHOUT THE summer, Tribble's feet and legs continued to hurt, but he still had not seen a doctor since his fall, mostly because he had never understood some of the ground rules of his employment. If his physical condition continued to decline, he knew he would have to stop working and go on disability, but the procedure by which that would happen was a mystery. Someone had told him that only the company's doctor could make the determination, and because the safety officer seemingly did not want him to see the doctor, Tribble was afraid that seeing his own physician would lead to trouble. The other complicating factor was financial. On disability, he would be paid substantially less than what he made from working and not enough to pay his bills. His daughter and her two children still lived in his house, and he covered much of their living expenses as well as his own.

In addition to everything else, Tribble's hands had begun to cramp. Someone told him it was probably because of a lack of potassium, so he started eating lots of bananas, but that did not have any effect. Then he wondered if he had arthritis and whether that was also affecting his legs. Regardless of the cause, by the end of most days, he was hobbling and in pain. "Every damn thing is going wrong," he said. "There are mornings when I say, 'What the hell am I doing?'"

Tribble was thinking about retiring. "I sort of have this feeling that I'm going down, if you know what I mean," he said after a particularly difficult day. He knew of only a handful of laborers at Trinity older than he was. "One guy is sixty-seven and one is about seventy, but I just don't know how a seventy-year-old guy can do it." Tribble's attitude was also deteriorating. For the first time in his life, he regularly spoke about missed opportunities and mortality. "When you get to sixty-two, you say, 'Damn, I should have gone to college and become a doctor or a lawyer or something.' But it's too late—it's getting to the part where it's all over."

Tribble also worried that he could not afford to retire. Even though he had been working for forty-three years, he would not be eligible for full Social Security benefits for another four years, when he would turn sixty-six. He also knew he was probably too old to find a different job except for a very low-paying one. "Some guys go out and pick up minimum-wage work at Wal-Mart, but that's all you can get," he said. And with the $7.25 minimum wage, his income would be well less than half of what it was at Trinity. If he were to rely on Social Security alone, his income would be about $1,200 a month, about $2,000 less than what he was earning. His savings were too modest to fill the gap. Having always spent money at basically the same rate as he earned it, his savings account contained just a couple of thousand dollars. He participated in Trinity's 401(k) program, but his account held less than $4,000.

If he waited until he was sixty-six, his Social Security payment would be about $1,600 a month. While he hated the idea of settling for the lower payment now, he was rethinking everything. "Here's the thing," he said. "What if I try to wait until I'm sixty-six, and I die before then? My wife is already dead, so the government would get to keep all my money. I've been paying money into this for a lot of years, and I don't want to lose it!"

While Tribble's financial circumstances were, of course, vastly different from Doug Von Allmen's, during the summer of 2010 the two men had arrived at a common realization: their present lifestyles were unsustainable. While Tribble's financial story had none of the dramatic ups and downs as Von Allmen's, money had become an overwhelming concern.

"I'm still trying to earn a living," Tribble said just before Labor Day weekend. "And I'm trying to live until I get out of there, if you know what I mean, but I'll probably still be working at Trinity Yachts when I die."

18

Bring on the Sun Beds

I know who you are, but you'll have to wipe your feet.
—Captain Richard Brown of the schooner *America*
to Prince Albert of England, 1851

Von Allmen's sufferings were less obvious—he spent much of the summer of 2010 cruising the Mediterranean aboard *Linda Lou*—but his financial concerns had led him to take a fateful step: he had listed *Lady Linda* with a broker as available for sale. Von Allmen had also decided that he would alter its design to broaden its appeal. He had, for example, asked Trinity to tell him what it would cost to create a locker near the swimming platform in which scuba diving equipment could be stored. The Von Allmens were not divers, but they knew it was an activity that appealed to many would-be yacht owners.

If circumstances were different, Von Allmen would have preferred to sell *Linda Lou* and retain *Lady Linda*. This was consistent with an age-old maxim that holds that boat owners find the vessel most appropriate for their needs only after they move up to one that is a size too large. For Von Allmen, *Linda Lou*'s biggest drawback was its cost. The new boat would be less expensive to operate because of its size and also because he could avoid dockage fees, which were typically $600 a day, by keeping it behind his house in Fort Lauderdale. And the convenience of setting out for cruises from his backyard was impossible to beat. With just a short stroll across the lawn and up the gangplank, his cruise could commence.

But Von Allmen was no longer in control of his yachting destiny. Given the slim likelihood that either boat would sell, he felt that he had no choice but to increase his chances of unloading one by offering both.

His efforts to sell *Linda Lou* had so far led to nothing but frustration. On the way to Abu Dhabi, where it went to be part of a boat show, it had been attacked by armed pirates. While they were unsuccessful, the boat subsequently had to be protected by barbed wire and armed guards. During the show, a member of Qatar's royal family offered to buy the yacht for $68 million, but when Von Allmen countered at $72 million, the prince lost interest. Since then, Von Allmen had received two other tentative offers, but they were at amounts that only slightly exceeded the vessel's $50 million cost. He rejected them out of hand, and when he attempted to contact the prince again, he heard nothing back. In September *Linda Lou* would go to the annual boat show in Monaco, which was, after Fort Lauderdale, the world's premier showcase for very large yachts.

Finding a buyer for *Lady Linda* while it was under construction was even less likely. After all, the main reason people go to the trouble of building a new vessel is the opportunity to make it uniquely their own. Without that, it is far easier and faster to buy one that is already completed. And with *Lady Linda* so far down the track, most of the big decisions had already been made. The shape of the hull was totally locked in, and so too was the interior layout. Much of the interior woodwork had been completed already and was on its way to Gulfport. The hardware for doors and drawers had been selected and ordered, and that was also true for the bathroom fixtures. A new owner could select the marble, the non-built-in, or "loose," furniture, and things such as crystal and cutlery, but that would not be enough for most. What's more, given the current state of the market, an existing yacht could be had for less money. The glory days of yachts being worth more than the cost of their construction were disappearing. Now the reverse was becoming the rule.

So it was a surprise when one of Trinity's best customers, an extraordinarily successful car dealer named Gene Reed, stepped forward to say he wanted to buy *Lady Linda*. A seventy-two-year-old native of Tennessee, Reed had a long history of buying and selling boats: thirty-six to date. Because most of his dealerships sold Chevrolets, his three most recent boats, all of them built by Trinity, were each named *Chevy Toy*. The first, which was delivered in 2000, was 118 feet long; the second, 142; and the third, which he still owned but was eager to replace, was 157. "They all seem big at first," he explained, "but if you like boats, as your wealth grows, so does your boat."

Reed had made his fortune building up and selling a string of dealerships in the southeastern United States, and he had recently agreed to sell a pair of South Carolina dealerships for $70 million, so he decided it was time for another step up. He wanted a new boat but did not want to wait out an entire building process, and he had ruled out buying a foreign-made yacht. "I made my money in America, and this is where I want to spend it," he explained. For Von Allmen, the stars seemed to have come into alignment to make an unlikely transaction possible. *Lady Linda* was the size Reed wanted, and he liked what he had seen of its design. Indeed, in every respect that was important to him, *Lady Linda* fit the bill. To some extent, this was because he was what yacht brokers termed a "wash-and-wear" buyer: someone not so focused as most on matters of design and decoration that he wanted to go to the trouble of customizing things. And since he wasn't married, there was no one else to weigh in, either.

But the transaction Reed proposed had a complicating twist: he wanted Von Allmen to take the 157-foot *Chevy Toy* in trade. Ironically, that would leave Von Allmen with a boat of exactly the same length as the one he had handed back to Trinity. And he would still end up owning two very large yachts, at least one more than he wanted. Even so, Von Allmen decided to pursue the deal. Since *Lady Linda* was much more valuable than *Chevy Toy,* he would receive a substantial sum of money as part of the trade. And given the diminished times, Von Allmen thought *Chevy Toy* might be about right for his future needs. While it would not command the presence of a larger yacht, it could be accommodated readily by the dock behind his house and could carry almost as many guests as *Lady Linda* or *Linda Lou.*

There was, however, a further complication, which became all too apparent after Von Allmen flew to Nantucket to see *Chevy Toy*: its dark-wood interiors gave it a look he described as "early bordello." Von Allmen decided to go forward with the deal anyway. Although he still would have to overcome the declining market to sell either *Linda Lou* or *Chevy Toy,* he decided it would be easier to sell *Chevy Toy,* which he judged to be worth about $16 million, than the partially constructed *Lady Linda*. Before he left Nantucket, he and Reed shook hands on the deal. The only major contingency was a thoroughgoing inspection that Reed scheduled for the following week in a Connecticut shipyard.

The inspection went well, revealing no major problems—but the trade was not to be. On the last day of August, John Dane sent an email to Von Allmen, who was still cruising the Mediterranean aboard *Linda Lou* when it arrived. "Bad news," Dane wrote. "Gene Reed just called and said Bank of America turned down his loan request. He is ticked off and is walking away from the purchase/swap." Reed had planned to finance part of the cost of acquiring *Lady Linda* with borrowed money, and the bank, which had provided him with loans for several of his other boats, had apparently declined to give him one now.

This left Von Allmen with more decisions to make. Trinity had submitted several proposed change orders for *Lady Linda* that he had ignored while he was negotiating with Reed. Now he had to decide whether to accept or reject them. Each one would require an upcharge. Von Allmen said yes to $9,378.88 for a waterproof door that was needed for the diving compartment, but no to the $20,377 that Trinity said it would cost to paint the locker's interior and equip it with a drain, a vent, and a light fixture; he thought he could have that work done less expensively somewhere else. He also said no to the $13,950 it would cost to add radiant heat panels above the table on the very top deck—the fly bridge—and $50,879 to add air-conditioning to the semienclosed space on that level.

IN MID-SEPTEMBER *Linda Lou* entered Monaco's crowded harbor with the Von Allmens on board. On the second day of the city-state's boat show, September 23, they met with Evan Marshall and John Dane to talk about other possible alterations to *Lady Linda*'s design.

A few minutes before the start of the meeting, Dane spoke to Marshall about yet another possible scenario for Von Allmen's future as a yacht owner. Dane had been attempting to persuade Von Allmen that he should sell *Lady Linda* and build another new yacht, one that would be smaller and less costly to operate. "Listen," he said to Marshall, "what we *really* need to do is to help Doug sell this boat because if he finds a buyer, I think he will build another boat. That would be good for you, and it would be good for us."

A few minutes later, Von Allmen explained his latest thinking: "We're probably not going to be able to sell *Lady Linda,* at least not until it's complete. And if we end up keeping it after that, we are going to be chartering it as much as we can, so I'd like to do some brainstorming on how we can maximize its appeal."

There was only so much that could be done. To guarantee interest in the charter market, a yacht its size should have a helipad, an

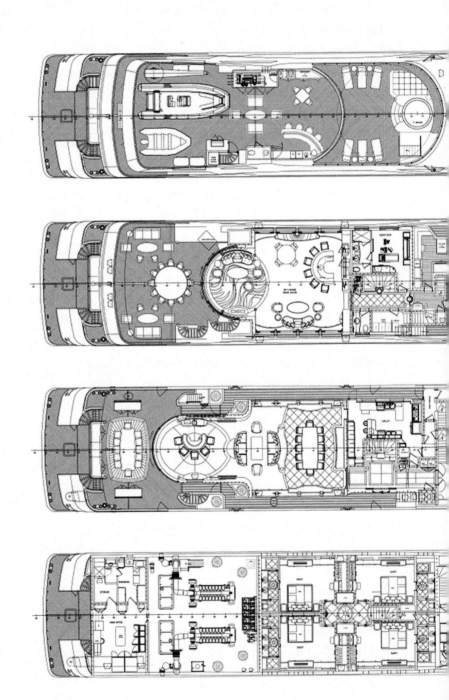

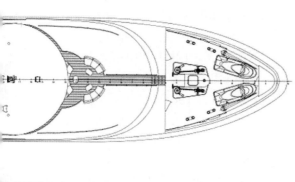

Fly bridge deck

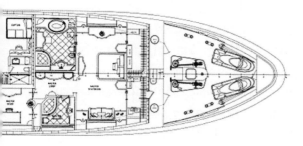

Sky lounge deck

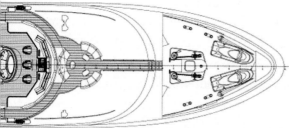

Main deck

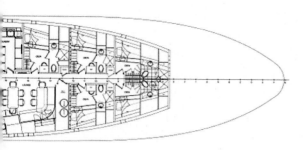

Guest stateroom deck

elevator, and a garage, but it was too late to add any of those features. Marshall did have other ideas. On the fly bridge, he said, there should be more seating. A Jacuzzi had always been part of the plan for that deck, and during the initial design phase Marshall had said it should be flanked by a pair of large "sun beds," platforms that would be covered with cushions and pillows. Von Allmen had said no, explaining that he and Linda would never use them, but now Marshall renewed his pitch: "Sun beds are kind of standard for a space like this."

Nodding, Von Allmen said, "Okay, okay, I'm fine with that."

Unwinding a roll of plans, Marshall pulled out one that showed the layout for the sky lounge. "We also need more furniture here," he said. A few weeks earlier, Von Allmen had decided not to buy a grand piano for the space. Marshall had recommended that it be replaced by some kind of furniture arrangement, but Von Allmen had wanted to leave it open. Now Marshall recommended filling the void with a sofa and a pair of lounge chairs that would surround an oval-shaped coffee table. Von Allmen agreed. Then he moved the conversation to costs. The carpeting would be synthetic, not wool, he said. Synthetics cost less and are easier to clean, an important consideration for a yacht that would be chartered. Von Allmen had already told Marshall he wanted to scale back on the marble and other stone that would be used for floors and in *Lady Linda*'s ten bathrooms. Marshall had originally thought the Von Allmens would spend more than $1 million for the stonework, but he had recently secured a $710,000 proposal from the Seattle-based company that had done the work on Von Allmen's 157-footer. Marshall said the firm had bid aggressively because it was loaded with excess inventory and that the Von Allmens could select anything they wanted from its warehouse.

They also talked about the *Chariot of Aurora* relief that was planned for the entry foyer. "Do you still want to spend one hundred thousand dollars for that?" Marshall asked. Although he had not gotten around to soliciting estimates from artists, he thought that was a reasonable guess for commissioning a multipaneled version of the Art Deco masterpiece that would have to be carved, painted, and gilded.

"I don't think so," Von Allmen said. "But if we don't do that, we would have to do something else to cover those walls."

Eager to preserve one of the signature features of *Lady Linda*'s design, Marshall suggested that the same image could be rendered as a mural rather than a three-dimensional relief. "We could still make a beautiful impression of what was on the *Normandie,* but it would cost a lot less. Maybe around fifteen thousand dollars."

"That sounds about right," Von Allmen said.

19

Smooth but Unlawful

We may have all come on different ships, but we're in the same boat now.

—Dr. Martin Luther King Jr.

By September 2010, *Lady Linda* was hidden from view. Scaffolding had been erected on every side, and the towering structure was covered with opaque sheets of plastic. The giant wrapper was supposed to protect Trinity's employees from fumes and dust now that the outside surfaces of the vessel were being sculpted and sanded. For the crew doing the work—eleven Hispanic men who were inside the plastic barrier—it had the opposite effect.

The critical ingredient to their work was a material they called putty but was in fact "fairing compound," an epoxy-based product that would cover every inch of *Lady Linda*'s exterior. It was surprisingly expensive, more than $70 a gallon, but because it could be made to take any shape, it facilitated near-miraculous transformations. Uneven surfaces could be made flat, awkward angles could be replaced by gentle radiuses. In the end, the aluminum plates that formed the hull and superstructure would become a single curvaceous form, and the finished surfaces would have the smoothness of porcelain.

It was because of that smooth uniformity that many people assume yachts like *Lady Linda* are made of fiberglass and born from giant molds. The glossy white paint that ultimately would cover Von Allmen's yacht would no doubt further that impression. And, in fact, because of the fairing compound and the polyurethane paint, *Lady Linda*'s skin would be a plastic-like amalgam. The materials would eliminate all evidence of the aluminum structure beneath.

The skills required to apply the fairing compound were not of the same order as Gale Tribble's, but the degree of labor intensity was even greater, and the work was dangerous—more dangerous, in fact, than any other aspect of the building process.

OSLY HEINANDEZ, a native of Honduras, had been assigned to a ten-foot-long section of the superstructure just beneath the windows of Von Allmen's study. Heinandez was twenty-one, but with a round face and smooth skin that did not require daily shaving, he looked even younger. He was just five foot seven but powerfully built, and he climbed up and down the scaffolding with the easy confidence of a natural athlete.

The fairing compound consisted of two ingredients, each of which came in five-gallon drums, and the first step was mixing them together. Kneeling on the scaffolding's metal planking, Heinandez scooped out equal quantities of each component and dumped them onto a piece of plywood. One of the ingredients was white and the other blue, and the standard for mixing them was to eliminate every trace of the original colors. Working the gunk together with a putty knife, Heinandez was careful not to be too vigorous because that could create air pockets that would result in finish-marring blisters. On the other hand, he could not take too long because he had only about forty-five minutes before the putty hardened to the point that it would no longer accommodate his wishes.

Once he judged the mixing to be complete, Heinandez lifted two or three pounds of it onto a smaller piece of plywood that would function like a painter's palette. Placing a small amount on the face of a broad putty knife, he spread a thin layer on the side of *Lady Linda*. It was something like icing a cake, although the material had the consistency of peanut butter and Heinandez's motions more closely resembled those of a plasterer. His objective was to make this section of the superstructure perfectly flat, while using the least amount of putty. Some areas were so depressed that he had to apply a half inch of putty, but other places required only an eighth of an inch or less. Thin slats of wood were glued to the metal in some places to provide a guide, but his work was mostly instinctive. And the results were soon apparent: low points, welding joints, and other imperfections disappeared, and the silver gray of the metal was replaced by bluish white.

Heinandez knew the fairing compound was dangerous. As soon as he pried open the tops of the containers, a strong odor not unlike that of paint thinner permeated the air. Those vapors were hazardous, but once the materials were combined, the chemical process that commenced generated fumes that were far worse. They smelled like nothing he recognized from outside the shipyard, and on the occasions when they permeated the mask he was wearing, he understood that a poison had entered his breathing passages. This happened regularly, and after four and a half years of fairing yachts, his health had suffered. On days when he worked with putty, Heinandez frequently developed a headache. Sometimes he felt dizzy, as if he were drunk, and on those days, he knew he would have trouble sleeping at night. Pinching his nose between his fingers, he explained, "I wake up feeling like everything is closed up." An avid soccer player since early childhood, Heinandez said he could no longer play for more than thirty minutes without feeling short of breath.

Two years earlier, a doctor had given Heinandez a prescription for a nasal spray that made it easier to breathe, but the doctor also urged him to find a different line of work. "He said, 'This stuff can kill you,'" Heinandez remembered. But he did not take the career advice. This was the only job he had ever had, and he did not think he could find another, particularly after the economy got into trouble. "I don't have any choices," he said.

The manufacturer of the fairing compound, DuPont, acknowledged the dangers. In an information sheet it provided to customers, it said the fumes "may cause nervous system depression, characterized by the following progressive steps: headache, dizziness, nausea, staggering gait, confusion, unconsciousness." It said symptoms included "shortness of breath, wheezing, cough, or permanent lung sensitization." Noting that irreparable lung damage could result, DuPont warned that anyone who had experienced "breathing problems" should not be exposed further to the product.

Heinandez should have been protected by the face mask he generally wore. However, for that to happen, the carbon-based filter that scrubbed toxic matter from the air had to be replaced frequently. Many boatyards provided fresh filters every day. Heinandez said his employer—a subcontractor hired by Trinity—expected workers to use the same filter for a week or longer. Whenever he smelled the putty, he knew the filter was no longer doing its job.

Heinandez admitted that he himself bore some responsibility for his health problems. When he first started working, he sometimes did not even bother to wear a mask. "I thought I was young and that I would not be working here that long, so it wouldn't matter," he said. He was much more careful now, although he said there was only so much he could do without an effective filter. His predicament left him with deeply ambivalent feelings. His job had changed his life, affording him a lifestyle that would not have been remotely possible in Honduras. On the other hand, the thought that his employer was trading away his health for profits was infuriating: "They know we're desperate," he said, "and they don't care what happens to us in the future."

There was also another factor. Like many of the men who were fairing *Lady Linda,* Heinandez's ability to complain, or find a different job, or even ask for advice was compromised by his status: he was an illegal immigrant.

A young immigrant from Honduras, Osly Heinandez,
sculpted *Lady Linda*'s exterior.

HEINANDEZ GREW up in a mountainous area of Honduras that rarely held on to its youth. He attended a nearby school when he was young, but because the closest high school was two hours away by bus and it required parents to buy costly books and supplies, his formal education ended when he was fifteen. After that, he helped his father, who operated a small automotive repair shop, but there was not enough work for both of them.

A relative who was a few years older had entered the United States illegally a few years earlier, and Heinandez resolved that he would too. Shortly after he turned sixteen, he paid $200 to be taken to the Mexican-American border. It was an uncomfortable thirty-day odyssey aboard ten different buses that traveled on back roads and at night to avoid detection by police who might demand travel documents and bribes. Once he reached the Rio Grande, he paid another $200 for a late-night trip across the river aboard a small boat, which was met by a van that delivered him to Laredo, Texas. His relative was working there as a housepainter, but Heinandez could not find a job. He thought about returning home but instead boarded a Greyhound bus that took him to Gulfport, where a cousin was working for one of three subcontractors that were fairing yachts at Trinity.

The thrill that came from securing a dollar-paying job was short lived. New employees were required to do nothing but sand fairing compound after it cured—the most physically taxing part of the process. In Heinandez's case, this went on for the first three months of his employment. "My arms hurt so much that I didn't think I was going to make it," he remembered. Pointing to his now substantial biceps, he added, "I eventually made my body stronger, and I became okay with it."

Heinandez had also come to grips with the reality that he, like many illegal immigrants, had entered the United States with unrealistic expectations. His initial plan was to spend two years in the country and then return home with enough money to expand his father's business so it could support both of them. That changed as he discovered how difficult it was to accumulate savings from his wages—he was paid $10 per hour plus an additional $5 for overtime—and also because of a chance encounter at a Circuit City store. He had purchased a car to get back and forth from work, and one of his colleagues gave him a pair of speakers, which Heinandez wanted to connect to the car's radio. When he went to the store to find an amplifier, Heinandez, who spoke almost no English, could not find what he needed until a bilingual twenty-six-year-old named Crystal offered to help. A cheerful woman with blue-green eyes and thick strawberry-blonde hair, she worked as a dispatcher for an air-conditioning repair company. A relationship developed, and they wed one year later, just before their son, Jayden, was born.

Now proficient in English, Heinandez shared an attractive three-bedroom house with his wife and Jayden, as well as two children from Crystal's previous marriage. Heinandez's base hourly wage had increased to $16, and he sent $400 to his parents every month, but he was committed to staying in the United States. "I'm leading an American life now," he said. "When I speak Spanish in the house, it feels odd. Even my dreams are in English."

Because of his marriage, Heinandez was theoretically entitled to residency. However, according to the law, he was required to return to his home country and then apply for an entry visa. Aware that other young men in exactly the same predicament had gone back home only to be rejected, he was unwilling to take the risk. "I could lose everything: my wife, my son, my job, my chance for a better life," he said after work one day. As his eyes overflowed with tears, he declared, "I just can't do it." Instead, he lived in constant fear. Since he did not have a valid driver's license, driving was a particular concern. He avoided highways, where officers of the Mississippi Highway Patrol were ubiquitous in their white SUVs, but he knew that even a parking lot accident or a minor traffic-law infraction could lead to a catastrophic encounter with the law. "If I see a cop, I'm scared," he said. "To tell you the truth, I'm *always* scared."

In addition to his legal and health worries, Heinandez also feared his job might disappear. During the boom times, there was so much fairing to be done that he sometimes worked more than eighty hours a week. In those days, he received bonuses when yachts were completed: $700 for one and $400 for another. Now there were no bonuses, and overtime was less frequent. "Everyone knows Trinity hasn't sold a boat in a long time," he said.

WHILE HEINANDEZ was creating *Lady Linda*'s skin, Billy Smith was talking about the yachting marketplace from behind his cluttered desk. "Of yachts forty meters or larger in the world today, thirty-eight percent of them are for sale," he said. "That's down a bit from what it was a year ago, but it's still far too high." The chief salesman did not mention another statistic that, for Trinity, was even more worrying: almost all of the yachts it had completed in the past couple of years were up for sale. He preferred to focus on more favorable big-picture economic fundamentals. "You have to have a net worth of something like two hundred fifty million dollars to own one of these boats," he said. "And if you look at the people in the world who have that much money today, just two and a half percent of them have a large yacht."

According to Smith, the greatest obstacle to Trinity's recovery was Barack Obama's big-spending instincts and the uncertainties that created for the entrepreneurial class that produced the bulk of Trinity's customers. "We've signed contracts to build sixty-one boats, and all but four of them have been with self-made people," he said. "They made their money doing all sorts of things: selling cars, crushing cars, making donuts, making furniture, pig farming, fire protection systems, lumber, check cashing, insurance, oil and gas. These are people who can deal with just about anything, but they cannot deal with uncertainty. They are not going to build a new boat when they're not sure if there'll be a fifty percent tax on yachts or if the dollar will become the peso."

Smith also cited another problem that, according to him, placed impossible burdens on the economy: illegal immigration. Seemingly unaware that some of the most difficult and dangerous work in his shipyard was being performed by undocumented workers, he added, "We *have* to protect our border. You're telling me we can put a man on the moon and we can't put up a fence? If you let these people in, they won't get a job. They will go on welfare because they can make more money that way than they can from working."

Every surface was covered with a highly toxic fairing compound.

ONE DAY after he applied fairing compound to the area of the hull outside Doug Von Allmen's study, Heinandez returned with an electric-powered circular sander. As the whirling abrasive made contact, a cloud of fine dust was launched. This too was dangerous. It was, as Heinandez put it, "the kind of stuff that goes in your lungs and doesn't come out."

As with the putty, he said, the filters for his mask were the problem. Dust-protecting filters were much less expensive than those required to stop chemical vapors, but they were supposed to be replaced every day. As with the vapor filters, he said his employer gave him a new one only once a week. "Whenever we complain about not getting new ones, the bosses say, 'If you don't like working here, the door is over there.'" Heinandez had recently given up asking and started buying his own filters, which cost $3 apiece; he inserted a new one into his mask every other day. But he said he could not afford to buy the carbon filters that would protect him from the putty fumes because they cost $25 each.

Heinandez would add five or six more layers of putty to the area he was working on, sanding after each application. The process would continue until every imperfection disappeared and the surface was perfectly straight and uniformly smooth. Several applications of paint would also be followed by sanding, each time with a finer grade of abrasive.

Heinandez was employed by a company that was fairing four of the five projects then under way at Trinity. Brian Wiehle, one of two brothers who managed the business, said the company always provided employees with the appropriate safety equipment, and he blamed any lapses on employees who failed to wear their masks. He said he was unaware that some of them were illegal immigrants. Then he pointed out that it was difficult to find people who were willing to do the work: "It's really hard to do, and it's dirty. It's not the kind of thing anyone wants to do unless they don't have a choice."

Wiehle had assembled crews of two basic types: some were Hispanic, from Mexico and other Central American countries; the others were from Vietnam. "We're an equal opportunity employer," he said. "I'll hire anyone who thinks they can do the work. That includes white guys who are from around here, but they never work out. They try, but they don't last long."

The amount of manpower assigned to fair *Lady Linda* would have a direct effect on the timing of its completion. Wiehle said he was eager to speed the process by doubling the size of the crew assigned to the boat, but he was not sure when that would happen. Throughout the fall of 2010, Trinity's production managers gave him the impression that they wanted to focus their resources on yachts other than *Lady Linda*.

20

Forget the Green

It isn't that life ashore is distasteful to me. But life at sea is better.

—Sir Francis Drake

Eager to select the stone that would be used for *Lady Linda*'s bathrooms, floors, and countertops, the Von Allmens flew to Seattle on October 18, 2010. Evan Marshall, who had come from London, was already at the terminal when they arrived, as was Jeff Homchick, the owner of the firm that would provide and install the stone.

Von Allmen had booked a return flight for the following afternoon, and he wanted to make all of the selections by then. While the process usually took much longer, Marshall thought they had a good chance of succeeding because the Von Allmens were both there and they planned to limit their choices to what Homchick had in stock. In addition, given how little time they had budgeted for their visit, Marshall guessed they were now in something closer to let's-just-get-it-done mode.

Or maybe not: during the fifteen-minute drive to Homchick's warehouse, Linda didn't sound like she was seeking shortcuts, asking Marshall, "You have the fabrics, don't you?" Several months earlier, the two of them had spent two days looking at textiles for furniture and curtains, and they took samples of everything they liked. For this trip, Marshall had brought Azzura's wood samples but none of the fabrics. After all, while the woods were locked in, the fabrics were not, and Marshall believed it would be impossible to select stones if they limited themselves to what matched both.

"No, I didn't bring them," he told Linda. "I didn't want us to get bogged down by them. Let's choose what we like here and then we can look at the fabrics again."

Obviously annoyed, Linda said, "I really wish you'd brought them."

During the ride, Von Allmen made it clear that he remained committed to the goal of using only unusual stones. "I could go quite a few years without seeing any more rain forest green," he said of a richly colored marble that had been popular in recent years.

Homchick's company was a small operation that did not have a showroom or a vast number of stones. But what it did have—about sixty types of marble and twenty onyxes—were the kinds of uncommon varieties that appealed to the Von Allmens. Large slabs leaned against steel frames in three warehouse rooms. Homchick was eager to do anything he could to please the Von Allmens. His company specialized in yachts and high-end houses, and now that the demand for both had plummeted, it had become much more difficult to turn his slabs into cash. He said he would mark the stones the Von Allmens selected on his clipboard and have them moved to a brightly lit space early on Tuesday. He also promised to gather a collection of "support stones" that complemented the Von Allmens' picks.

One of the stones Doug Von Allmen liked was a slab of "orange onyx." Composed of various shades of brown and orange, the colors created a striking pattern that conveyed a sense of motion, as if a stream of multicolor liquids had been captured in midflow.

A few months earlier, the Von Allmens had agreed that they would try to stay away from onyxes because they are more expensive than marble. But Von Allmen was drawn to several in Homchick's warehouse, and now that they had agreed to a fixed price, money was no longer an issue. By the end of the day, eight of the fifteen stones they had designated as possibilities were onyx, including "paradise onyx," which had striking straight-edged veins of purple.

On Von Allmen's previous yachts, the centers of each of the guest bathroom floors and walls were made with relatively inexpensive "filler stones": the same one in each bathroom, and bordered by more interesting stones. But on this one, he wanted each bathroom to be completely different and did not want to use a filler stone in any of them. "It's a forty-million-dollar boat," he said. "I don't think we can cut corners."

Surprised by Von Allmen's positive frame of mind, Marshall guessed that something had happened to improve his financial outlook, and his instinct was correct: several potential buyers for *Linda Lou* had emerged recently, and Von Allmen hoped to conclude a sale with one of them by the middle of November. If he was successful, the Von Allmens were more likely to keep *Lady Linda*.

But uncertainties remained. All of the potential buyers were Russian, and that gave Von Allmen reason to be wary. "Almost all of the real buyers right now are Russian," he observed. "The Arabs are active but much less so, and *no one* is buying in the US. But the Russians are so volatile that it's impossible to count on them until they deliver the money." Financial capacity was not the problem. Von Allmen had finalized the sale of his New York apartment to a Russian, and one of his friends had sold a yacht to a Russian who delivered the purchase price, close to $40 million, in suitcases of $100 bills. "Some of the buyers are politicians," he explained. "They put the boats in their wives' names."

Although he laughed about the scale of corruption in Russia, Von Allmen was not at all amused by the political scene in the United States. Like Billy Smith, he put undocumented immigrants near the top of his list of concerns. "It's great to be charitable to illegal aliens and others who don't add anything to the economy, but we can't afford that anymore. If you look at the family budget, and there's more going out than coming in, do you give a lot of money to charity? Of course not! Why should the government behave any differently?" Unaware of the role illegal immigrants were playing in constructing *Lady Linda,* Von Allmen added, "None of this makes much difference to me, but it will kill what made this country great."

BY THE time they reconvened at Homchick's warehouse the next morning, all of the slabs the Von Allmens liked and several others that Homchick had chosen had been gathered in one place. Happy with most of them, they selected "light honey onyx" for the floor of the main salon and the foyer. That stone would be framed with a border made from two of Homchick's choices, both of them brown-tinged onyxes: "light caramel" and "dark caramel." The Von Allmens apportioned the rest of the stones, one room at a time, without any real disagreement or difficulty, and in just a couple of hours, they were done. Marshall was pleased. Even though the choices had been made quickly, he felt like there had been no compromises or disappointments. And as they headed back to the airport, he was also pleased that the Von Allmens seemed to be approaching the project with a renewed sense of enthusiasm.

An array of important decisions remained, including the loose furniture (budgeted at $200,000), carpeting ($100,000), upholstery ($60,000), window treatments ($55,000), mirrors ($50,000), and bedspreads ($40,000). If the Von Allmens were still willing to spend the budgeted amounts, Marshall thought the selection process should not be difficult. And for him, it would also be profitable because he would earn a fee equal to 22 percent of what was spent, in addition to what he was paid for designing the yacht itself. Marshall, who was, of course, eager to see the project through to completion, also knew that the stone selections, by further limiting what another owner could do to customize the yacht, would decrease the chances of *Lady Linda* being sold during its construction.

21

A Box Within a Box

Never in my life before have I experienced such beauty, and
fear at the same time. Ten icebergs so far today.

—TWENTY-FOUR-YEAR-OLD ELLEN MACARTHUR, WHO
SINGLE-HANDEDLY SAILED AROUND THE WORLD IN 2001

NO ONE was more familiar with *Lady Linda*'s interior than Geoff
Demaere, who was managing Azzura Marine's nine-man crew in
Gulfport. By the fall of 2010, they had spent several months preparing
to install the paneling and furniture that had been made in Australia,
but they did not have much to show for their effort.

It made no sense to install paneling that would have to be
dismantled later because some other kind of work had yet to be
done—and there were obstacles in every compartment. In the main
salon, an overhead pipe stretched halfway across the ceiling but then
stopped, obviously in need of a connecting length of pipe. Some of
the pipes had been marked with stickers indicating that they had
been inspected and pressure tested, but others had not. A structural column had been welded in a location that made it impossible
to install a decorative one. In the master stateroom, none of the
required fire sprinklers had been hooked up, several electrical junc-
tion boxes still had to be mounted behind walls, and there were no

wires leading to the wall-mounted television or the two televisions that would be concealed within the mirrors in the Von Allmens' bathrooms.

As an outside contractor, there was a limit to what Demaere could do. "I can advise my company on what the problems are, and I can tell Trinity what needs to be done," he explained, "but I have to rely on others to make a lot of things happen."

A compact forty-nine-year-old with a military officer's demeanor, Demaere had spent so much time inside *Lady Linda* that he could find his way around with his eyes closed. Indeed, he knew its interior spaces so intimately that he had identified several flaws in their design—and that too was problematic. In the master stateroom, he was, according to the plans, supposed to build out the walls in a way that would seal off several cubic feet of space that could otherwise be added to each of the Von Allmens' wardrobe closets. In the sky lounge, the cabinets that would line either side of the room were designed to be about a foot deep, but that dimension could be almost doubled in some places if the backs of the cabinets were extended to reach closer to the hull.

Demaere assumed—no doubt correctly—that Von Allmen would prefer to utilize the gaps. "It's Evan Marshall's design, and Trinity approved the plans, but it's a mistake," Demaere said. "The space is too valuable to waste. And if the owner finds out what happened, who is going to suffer the consequences? We would. We would have to undo our work and do it all over again."

WITH WOOD harvested from Eastern Europe and cabinetry designed in London and built in Australia before it was shipped to Mississippi, *Lady Linda*'s interior was a global enterprise. Demaere's background was equally international. Born in Belgium, he grew up in Africa, where his grandparents were farmers and his father worked for a mining company. He returned to Belgium to learn how to make furniture at a technical school but then returned to Africa to teach at a high school in Cameroon. Attracted to Australia because it had the open spaces of Africa but far greater political stability, he emigrated there in 1990 and established a furniture-making business. He started working on yachts when one of his customers commissioned a 100-foot boat.

Working in Gulfport was a hardship. Rather than living with his wife and four children, he shared an apartment with two members of his crew—an arrangement that made it seem like his workday never really ended. For perfection-minded cabinetmakers, the apartment itself, on the third-floor of a garden apartment building just a few miles from the yard, was also a bit hard to take. Arriving there after work one day, Andrew "Skippy" Pratt, one of Demaere's apartment mates, said, "Whenever I look at this kitchen, I say, 'Why are all the hinges in different places? Why isn't the countertop level? And why does one of the drawers not have a knob?'"

Managing a group of young men, most of them in their twenties and thirties, who did not want to be in southern Mississippi, was also challenging. "Most of the guys want to go home, and that has an impact on the job," said Demaere. Running an operation so far from home was also expensive. Azzura rented four apartments, each costing $980 a month, and it also had to buy two vans to transport everyone to and from the yard. And because most of the men entered the United States on short-term visas, they had to leave the country every three months. The travel and lost time were two more major expenses—and Demaere was never sure whether members of his crew would return. Standing in one of *Lady Linda*'s guest staterooms, he said, "Nothing is happening here because the guy who was doing the work had to go back to Australia to renew his visa." Motioning toward the adjacent guest stateroom, he added, "The same thing will happen in this cabin next week." Of Azzura's executives back in Australia, he remarked, "I don't think they knew what we were getting into."

Azzura's employees were appalled by the working conditions at Trinity. The divide between blue-collar workers and supervisors seemed much greater than it is in Australia, and the cabinetmakers saw that as being not just unpleasant but also counterproductive. "The toilets are totally disgusting," Marty Turk, one of Azzura's employees, said of the bathrooms used by laborers. Turk, a twenty-six-year-old who had a stainless-steel piercing through the left side of his lower lip, was also troubled by how laborers were required to pass through the security gate, where they punched the time clock and had their lunch pails inspected. "We have time clocks at home, but they're there to keep track of the number of hours we work on a project," he said. "Here it's because they don't trust anyone." Turk believed Trinity's approach contributed to what he considered to be a horrible work ethic among its laborers. "A lot of the guys here are incredibly lazy," he claimed. "You could get rid of a third of them, and I don't think it would slow things down very much."

SKIPPY PRATT was the only Azzura employee who enjoyed living in Gulfport. He had been there before. In 2006, while working for a different company, he had worked on the interior of *Unbridled,* another Trinity yacht, which had been built for Bill Wrigley Jr., the chairman of his family's chewing gum and candy company (and one of the very small number of Trinity customers who had inherited wealth). Pratt, who grew up on a farm in the Australian outback, liked to fish, and he had recently bought his own car and a small boat for hunting bass on weekends. "You have to make the most of it," he said.

On *Lady Linda,* he was assigned to the bridge. His first task was leveling the floor, which was accomplished by building a lattice of wooden slats of varying heights on the metal decking. The lowest point had to be raised by almost two inches to be equal to the highest. After using a laser to confirm that the slats were where they needed to be, he glued thin strips of rubber to the top of each of them. Structural components of large vessels inevitably shift and twist, and the rubber was part of an elaborate strategy for absorbing the movements, the first step in creating what essentially would be a floating box within the metal structure: a box containing the finished walls, floors, and ceilings. In addition to preventing interior walls and moldings from cracking or breaking, this approach would hinder the conductivity of sound.

Once the rubber strips were in place, Pratt laid down what is called an acoustic floor: plywood that incorporates a sound-deadening six-millimeter layer of rubber. To that he glued the copy sole: panels of marine plywood that had been marked to show furniture locations in exactly the same way as the floor in Azzura's mockup back in Australia. Later on, the finished floor, which would be made of two-inch-wide strips of teak and much thinner ones of holly, would be glued to the top of the copy sole.

Pratt was now working on the ceiling. Like the floor, it would not be connected directly to the metal frames above. Instead, more than fifty hangers would be attached to the frames. The height of the hangers could be adjusted, and they had rubber joints to limit movements of the superstructure from affecting the finished ceiling. Pratt said it would take about three weeks to install all of the hangers and get their levels exactly right. Once that was done, the hangers would hold the "rough-in": sections of plywood, which, like the floor, incorporated a rubber acoustic lining. The final ceiling, made from fabric-covered panels, would then be clipped to the rough-in. The rough-in panels would also be used for the construction of the walls. They would be attached to the ceiling and the floor but not to the superstructure of the yacht itself.

Pratt enjoyed his job. Uninterested in going back to work on his family farm, he hoped it would become a permanent career. His only complaint was the poor quality of the air he was breathing. Osly Heinandez's colleagues were operating electric sanders just outside, and none of the glass windows that would wrap around the front and sides of the bridge had been installed. Sheets of plastic had been placed over the window frames in an attempt to keep the dust outside, but the effort was less than fully successful. Pratt understood how dangerous the dust was—and also how much worse it was for Heinandez and the others outside. "What they do is totally nuts," he said. "I'd rather pick up rubbish than do what they do."

After Pratt completed the rough-in work in the bridge, there was nothing else he could do there. Like elsewhere, the obstacles were obvious. None of the wiring to the navigational equipment had been installed. Inch-thick cables that would link the bridge to the engine room were lying on the floor in coiled heaps. A "close-out" form posted on a wall near the entrance provided documentary evidence of what still needed to be accomplished. A supervisor for each of the major trades—electricians, pipefitters, and shipfitters—as well as a Trinity foreman and someone from the quality control department, had to sign his name in a designated box before Azzura could be confident that the finished panels could be installed. In the bridge, every one of the boxes was empty. "It's a good system," Pratt said of the forms. "Down the road, if Trinity tells us they forgot to install some pipes, we can say, 'Yes, well, but you marked right here that you were done.'" But for now, it demonstrated that Pratt was about to reach a bottleneck.

AZZURA AS a whole also was heading toward a bottleneck—or worse. The only finished wood that had been installed anywhere on the yacht was the crown moldings that Richard Meester had painstakingly cut seven months earlier, and even they had not been secured permanently. Demaere was holding off on that until the nearby air-conditioning vents and pipes were tested. "That molding weighs more than three hundred pounds," he explained. "Once it's glued up there, you don't want to have to try to get it down again."

Because so little of its work had been completed, Azzura was in a serious financial bind. "Trinity is supposed to pay us progress payments based on what's completed so far," Demaere explained. "But for that to happen, I have to prove that things are one hundred percent done—and *nothing* has gotten to that point." Worse still, *Lady Linda* remained Azzura's only project. "If we don't come up with something else soon, Azzura could just disappear," Demaere said.

A couple of weeks before Christmas 2010, a container carrying the furniture for the guest staterooms, including the bedside table Mitch Davies and Travis Brown had made, was scheduled to reach Gulfport. But that did not necessarily mean progress would accelerate. "I hope we can start to really put things together in January," Demaere said, "but it doesn't look like Trinity is going to be ready for us."

22

It's Not My Fault

Each man makes his own shipwreck.

—ATTRIBUTED TO ROMAN POET
MARCUS ANNAEUS LUCANUS (AD 29–AD 65)

A COUPLE of weeks before Christmas 2010, just after ten in the morning, a plane, a Learjet 40 carrying Doug and Linda Von Allmen, touched down at a small airport just a few miles from Trinity's shipyard. Gale Tribble had begun *Lady Linda*'s construction almost three years earlier, but the Von Allmens were about to see it for the first time. It was a cold morning—deep-freeze warnings were the lead story on all of the local newscasts—and Von Allmen was wearing a black wool jacket over a navy blue sweater. Linda's dress, coat, and high-heeled boots were all black. She was also wearing an array of silver jewelry and a diamond-encrusted watch.

Billy Smith did not arrive at the airport to pick them up until after the plane had landed, so the Von Allmens were in the waiting room when he pulled up in his black SUV. They did not say they were annoyed, nor were they very sociable either once they settled into the backseat. Von Allmen pulled a cell phone out of his pocket and called his stepson to discuss an issue that had come up in connection with the Rothstein litigation. During and after the call, Von

Allmen flipped through a copy of *duPont Registry,* a magazine devoted to Ferraris and other sports cars. Linda was also talking on her cell phone, giving shipping instructions for Christmas presents that had to get to children from their previous marriages.

When a conversation with Smith did begin, it was framed by the weather, their shared political convictions, and what they believed to be overblown fears about global warming. "Have you ever noticed that Al Gore always seems to disappear around this part of the year?" Von Allmen quipped. He went on to criticize Barack Obama's efforts to stimulate the still-flagging economy, saying, "Half the jobs his stimulus program created were government jobs." To that, Smith added, "And none of the private sector jobs were in manufacturing."

Smith drove directly into the yard and parked just a few steps away from the stairs that led from the factory floor up to *Lady Linda*'s main deck. Linda led the way, followed by her husband, Smith, and Ingo Pfotenhauer, Von Allmen's project manager. When Von Allmen reached the main salon, he just stood there, not saying a word. He was furious, blown away by the obvious lack of progress. None of the finished walls and ceilings had been installed, so rather than seeing wood paneling and onyx floors, he was looking at unopened crates of cabinetry and unfinished walls within which tangles of wires were competing for space with insulation material that was covered with what looked like aluminum foil.

At various points during the construction process, he had been happy to accept delays because they slowed the rate at which he had to send progress payments to Trinity and he had another yacht, but now that he thought he was about to sell *Linda Lou,* he wanted *Lady Linda* to be delivered to him in time for the summer. He wanted to put it out for charter during the peak of the Mediterranean season, when brokers said he could charge $450,000 a week. He also wanted it for his own use, particularly for the days surrounding August 21, his seventieth birthday. Given what he saw now, that did not seem remotely possible. And as he stood on the dusty metal decking and

slowly turned in a full circle, he had already decided that the trip
to Gulfport was a complete waste of time. There were no decisions
to be made, and he was unable to evaluate what he saw in terms of
what the project would become. Everything was such a mess that
he could see only what still needed to be done. That he had spent
several thousand dollars to fly to Gulfport added to his frustration.

Linda's reaction was similar. "There's *no way* we are going to have
this boat by next summer," she whispered.

Walking toward the bow, Von Allmen passed through the main
salon and the entry foyer, still without saying anything, and then
into the master stateroom. Stopping at the space that would become
his study, he fixated on two plastic-covered gaps in the hull: a pair
of rounded rectangular shapes, both of them upright, that would
become windows. Not only was the glass not installed, but Von Allmen believed the gaps were in the wrong place.

"They're so low," he said.

"They are higher than what Evan originally drew," Pfotenhauer
said.

While the windows would be large, almost five feet high, their
highest point, for someone of Von Allmen's height, was barely above
eye level. "I won't be able to see the sky!" he said, referring to the
sightlines from where he was standing. Without saying anything
else, Von Allmen led the others into the next compartment, the bedroom itself.

Having seen the plans many times, the Von Allmens were, of
course, familiar with the layout. Inevitably, though, the first experience with any actual three-dimensional reality has its surprises. "It's
not as big as I thought it would be," Linda said. In fact, it was large—
thirteen by twenty-five feet—but she was looking at the markings
of the copy sole and focusing on particular dimensions that seemed
problematic. The thirty-nine inches that would separate the foot of
the king-sized bed and the bowed cabinet on the opposite wall did
not seem big enough. And the areas on either side of the bed seemed

overly generous; she worried that there would not be enough natural light in the center of the room. The windows were large, exactly the same as those in Von Allmen's study, but there were just four of them, two on each side. Von Allmen thought that they were, like the ones in his study, too low. Linda thought there should be more of them.

"Couldn't we have two more windows in here, one on each side?" she asked.

"You could; anything is possible," Pfotenhauer said. "But at this point, it would be *really* expensive."

Leaving the master stateroom without saying anything about that or anything else, Von Allmen returned to the foyer and descended a narrow set of stairs. Halfway down, he asked, "Is this where I should be going?"

Billy Smith, who was a couple of steps behind, replied, "This takes you down to the crew quarters."

Reversing course, Von Allmen said, "I don't need to go there."

Walking down the main stairs, Von Allmen entered one of the guest staterooms, where he was introduced to Geoff Demaere. Most of Trinity's workers had been told to get off the boat in advance of the Von Allmens' arrival, and many of Azzura's employees decided that they should do the same, but Demaere had stayed. Embarrassed that so little finished wood could be seen by the owner, he rushed to unwrap a desktop that had been made for the cabin. In his haste, he neglected to mention that the surface he was showing would be the desktop's *underside*—the top was to be marble—but no one picked up on the distinction. Of the wood's highly varnished light-toned finish, Von Allmen said, "It looks nice," but his tone was obviously halfhearted.

Returning to the main stairs, he went all the way up to the sky lounge level and into the compartment that was designed to function as both a gym and a stateroom. Given the mixed use, it was supposed to have a Murphy bed, which would be concealed behind what would look like bookshelves when it was not in use. However, now that Von Allmen planned to charter or sell the yacht, he was having second thoughts about the bed. Since most large yachts had five staterooms—a master stateroom plus four for guests—having *six* would go a long way to enhance its marketability. With a fold-down bed, he feared that this room would not really qualify.

"Why don't we make this a permanent bed," he suggested. It would be a significant change—Azzura's craftsmen had already spent hundreds of hours fabricating the Murphy bed and the cabinetry in which it would be contained—but no one objected.

Von Allmen appeared to be in a hurry. Leaving the rest of the group behind, he strode in and out of the wheelhouse too quickly to notice the flooring or the rough-ins that Skippy Pratt had completed. Just as quickly, he passed through the galley, which was entirely empty, before he reached the sky lounge. There he finally found something he liked.

"This is such a great space," he said with obvious enthusiasm. When someone mentioned the design flaw that Demaere had identified—how the cabinets on the sides of the room could be made to have much more interior space—Von Allmen agreed immediately that should be done, but his overall impression remained positive. He was also pleased with the outside deck just behind the sky lounge and the fly bridge deck that was above the sky lounge. But that was the end of his tour. The yacht would end up costing Von Allmen about $40 million, and he and Linda had devoted just forty minutes to inspecting its construction.

Back in Smith's car, Linda said, "I have to say our bedroom feels small."

"We don't live there," her husband replied. "We just sleep there."

"But it really seems tight."

"It's too late . . ."

THE NEXT stop was a large conference room where several Trinity executives had assembled, and it was there that Von Allmen asked the question that had been eating at him since he first stepped aboard *Lady Linda*.

"Let me ask you, isn't this boat supposed to be done in April?"

There was no response. Although he was as irritated by the silence almost as much as by what he had seen, Von Allmen repeated his question in the same modulated tone: "Aren't you supposed to deliver the boat to me in April?" In fact, according to his most recent revision to the contract, the delivery was supposed to be by March 15, 2011.

When someone finally spoke, it was Stuart McClure, who had recently become Trinity's project manager for *Lady Linda*. Before he came to Trinity, he had been the captain of a 265-foot yacht owned by Prince Khaled bin Sultan, Saudi Arabia's deputy defense minister and a nephew of the king, so he had plenty of experience deferring to the owner class. Now, as one of the least-senior executives in the room, he realized that it would be up to him to deliver the bad news.

"Yes, it's supposed to be done in April," he began. "But we have seen Azzura's shipment dates, and it looks like some of their furniture will not even get here until April."

Even now, Von Allmen did not raise his voice, but his disappointment became apparent. Following another uncomfortable silence, he asked, "Do you have an actual delivery date?"

Rather than answer the question, McClure introduced another complication, noting that Jeff Homchick could not install the marble countertops in the bathrooms and elsewhere until Azzura installed the vanities and cabinets on which they would rest.

Von Allmen tried again: "Do you have an anticipated delivery date?"

"You may want to shoot me," McClure replied, "but I'm going to say August or September."

Until now, Linda had been silent, but she was also annoyed, all the more so because she knew Trinity had a habit of launching yachts shortly before the all-important Fort Lauderdale boat show in October. "Just in time for the boat show," she deadpanned. "What a shocker."

Von Allmen tried a different approach: "Do you think we could get it done by my seventieth birthday: August 21?"

Once again, there was no substantive response. Not long after that, during the drive back to the airport in Billy Smith's SUV, Linda asked, "Billy, why is the boat *so* late?"

Smith pinned all of the blame on Azzura. "The furniture is very, very late—and, you know, there's a sequence to everything we do."

Von Allmen saw no point in challenging Smith, although he did point out the cost of the delay: "If I don't have the boat next summer, I'm going to miss the best chartering season, and that would probably cost me two million dollars."

"I'm really not sure how we got to this point," Smith said. "It's the first I've heard about it. I'll look into it and let you know." Fortunately for Smith, he had arrived at the airport by then. Driving onto the tarmac, he parked next to Von Allmen's plane and stepped outside to say good-bye. As the Von Allmens climbed the steps, Smith was obviously relieved. "What you just saw is very unusual," he remarked to someone who was standing nearby. "We just told a guy that he is not going to get his boat until after the summer is over—and he didn't go ballistic. Most owners would have gone *totally* ballistic!"

NEEDLESS TO say, Geoff Demaere would not have been happy if he knew his company was being blamed for the delays in *Lady Linda*'s construction. He would have pointed out that Azzura could not hire the craftsmen until Trinity funded the contract and that he could not install the products of their labor until Trinity completed its work.

One day after Von Allmen's visit, Demaere pointed to additional obstacles. In Von Allmen's study, he had just removed one of the rough-in panels that had been set up there, because a plumber needed to conduct a second pressure test on some of the air-conditioning pipes. "As soon as we install something, we have to take it off," Demaere said. In the master stateroom, a metal tray that had been hung above the ceiling to carry various kinds of wires was still empty. "We couldn't install furniture here even if it had arrived," he said. "In almost every part of the yacht, we have gone about as far as we can."

Demaere had been working on yachts long enough to know that every new build involved a blame game and that his team was at a distinct disadvantage because no one at Azzura had ever had any direct contact with *Lady Linda*'s owner beyond his fleeting encounter the day before. "Everyone always ends up blaming everyone else," he said, "but the end result is the same: the boat doesn't get done when it's supposed to."

23

We're Going Home!

To reach a port, we must sail—sail, not lie at anchor—
sail, not drift.

—Franklin Delano Roosevelt

THE PACE of *Lady Linda*'s construction remained painfully slow throughout the spring of 2011. Shortages of construction materials, even the most basic of them, were part of the problem. Electricians ran out of the plastic ties they used to bundle wires. Pipefitters sometimes could not find the cement with which they fastened lengths of PVC pipes to one another. Certain that Trinity's financial difficulties were to blame, Ingo Pfotenhauer worried that quality could suffer: "We've seen pipefitters using a mishmash of different screws and wires to mount pipes. These are pipes that won't be seen, but it reflects an inattention to detail that's troubling."

Major construction items were also missing. The windows—they are called portholes on most vessels, but *Lady Linda*'s were so large that the nautical convention was generally ignored—were a particular concern. To produce glass strong enough to withstand wind and sea, a company in New Zealand, Glasshape, would manu-facture half-inch-thick panels comprised of three layers: two sheets of glass that would be laminated to a core of virtually unbreakable plastic. The windows should have been installed months earlier, but none of them had even arrived in Gulfport. And until they were in place, Azzura Marine could not mount the nearby wall paneling because the first step was to frame the glass with molding. Here too, Pfotenhauer said, the issue was money. Because Trinity had been slow to send an initial payment to Glasshape, the windows would not arrive until June or July.

Progress on the other yachts still under way at Trinity was also slow, but none was creeping along as slowly as *Lady Linda*. One of the reasons was the $21 million credit Von Allmen had received for trading in his 157-footer. As Pfotenhauer put it, "If Trinity has a choice between working on *Lady Linda* or a boat that will result in them getting progress payments, which one do you think it's going to be?"

GEOFF DEMAERE did not know anything about Von Allmen's giant credit, but he, better than anyone, understood just how far behind schedule everything was. By now the close-out forms for every compartment should have been executed fully, but not one was complete. While Demaere had attempted to describe the situation to his colleagues in Australia, Azzura chief executive David McQueen was appalled by what he saw after he arrived in Gulfport on March 8. Although he recognized that most of the problems were beyond Demaere's control, he blamed him for not providing a better understanding of the sorry state of things, and McQueen fired him from the company. "There wasn't anything else I could have done," Demaere said afterward. "I was not in control of production."

Later that day, McQueen met with several Trinity executives and demanded a realistic schedule that would indicate when Azzura could install its woodwork. All of the close-out forms would be executed fully by March 31, he was told. On the basis of that, McQueen said Azzura's paneling and furniture would be put in place by the end of July—leaving, at least theoretically, enough time for Trinity to deliver *Lady Linda* to Von Allmen by his birthday. But when McQueen returned to the yard in early April, he saw that even the March 31 deadline had been missed. The close-out forms were complete for the guest staterooms but not for any of the other compartments.

McQueen tapped out an angry email to John Dane: "I have decided that it is better for Azzura Marine to bring home five trades-men and save their hours for the future completion of the job." Three or four Azzura employees would stay in Gulfport, but McQueen said the others would fly home to Australia as soon as flights could be booked. "When the job and the areas are more complete," he con-tinued, "I can bring the tradesmen back to the vessel."

In an immediate reply, Dane urged McQueen to reconsider, say-ing, "This is a big mistake on your part."

McQueen would not budge. "All of the agreed dates have been missed, and I do not have new dates to work with," he wrote. "We were/are wasting many hours not being productive." He told Dane he would make another trip to Gulfport on May 3 to once again assess Trinity's progress.

WHEN HE received an update on the troubling rate of progress, Von Allmen could not help himself from worrying about what he had come to regard as the nightmare scenario: that *Lady Linda* would fall so far behind that it would end up being one of the very last vessels in Trinity's dwindling production queue, increasing the chances that the company's financial difficulties would become totally incapaci-tating before his yacht made it across the finish line. Von Allmen also understood that his $21 million credit would soon be exhausted, so he would have to start sending cash to Trinity. According to Pfoten-hauer's assessment, *Lady Linda* was then close to 65 percent com-plete. Based on its approximate total cost of $40 million, that implied the cost to date was approaching $26 million. And that was equal to what Von Allmen had contributed thus far: the $21 million credit plus $5 million in cash payments.

While the carrot of progress payments would theoretically motivate Trinity to devote more resources to *Lady Linda,* Von Allmen did not want to send any money to the company until he had a better understanding of its financial position. In April 2011 he engaged an attorney, Albert Frevola, a partner at the law firm that was representing him in the Rothstein litigation, to investigate. Frevola gathered records and emails and spoke to David McQueen before he went to Gulfport. When he met with John Dane, the company's president assured him that he had a longstanding $30 million revolving line of credit from a Florida financial institution, Regent Bank. In recent years, he said, Trinity had drawn on the credit line to borrow as much as $25 million. But as of March 31, 2011, its borrowings were much less, $9.3 million. Assuming the line of credit remained in place, that meant Trinity had access to more than $20 million to fund its operations.

Encouraged by the news, Von Allmen sent Pfotenhauer an email, saying, "Your concerns are probably not merited."

Pfotenhauer was not convinced. He knew every loan agreement came with conditions. He did not know the specifics of this one, but they no doubt would be related to Trinity's financial health: its profitability or the value of its assets relative to the amount of its debt. If the covenants were violated, the bank could cancel the loan. "Trinity gave Doug a snow job," Pfotenhauer said later. "They owe money to almost everyone they do business with—that's like broadcasting to the yachting industry that you're in trouble. They wouldn't let that happen unless they were running out of options."

Evan Marshall was also skeptical. He had submitted dozens of invoices to Trinity for lighting fixtures and loose furniture that would be manufactured by various suppliers, most of them in Europe. Under its contract with Von Allmen, Trinity was required to pay for the furniture and the fixtures, but it had not sent Marshall the money he needed to pass along to the suppliers. By the end of April, the total amount of the outstanding invoices was close to $500,000. Marshall knew that the furniture makers would not start the work until they received deposits and that many of them shut down for the entire month of August. "If we don't get these companies going," Marshall said, "we're going to lose *a lot* more time—and Trinity is going to end up pointing the finger at me. They'll say, '*Lady Linda* isn't done because Evan took too long to place the furniture orders.'"

24

It's Not Just Copying

Ships are the nearest things to dreams that hands have
ever made.

—"The Song of a Ship," Robert N. Rose,

business executive and poet

In the spring of 2011, one of the elements still missing from *Lady Linda* was its version of *The Chariot of Aurora*. Carin Wagner, an artist in Florida, was struggling to get it done. Although she had been initially thrilled to have the opportunity, she had been having second thoughts ever since. For one thing, it would require at least twice the number of hours she had estimated when she told Evan Marshall she was willing to do the job for $15,000. And if she was going to meet the Labor Day deadline he had given her, she would have to work every day, weekends included, throughout the summer.

The arrival of the seventeen panels of high-density particleboard on which she would paint—the largest of which was eight feet long and weighed almost one hundred pounds—had set the tone. They were supposed to be delivered to her studio, a large, brightly lit room off the kitchen of her house. But it was raining when the truck arrived on the morning of June 2, and the driver refused to risk going down the unpaved driveway. He also made it clear that he was not going to assist with the unloading, so Wagner recruited a couple of neighborhood friends. For the next several hours, three women in flip-flops carried the inch-thick panels, one at a time, down from the truck, up the driveway, and into the studio.

The panels were numbered to indicate their eventual position in *Lady Linda*'s stairwell, but the first applications of paint did not require any particular arrangement. The finished work would be dominated by the golden sun and several large figures—six humans and seven horses—but the backgrounds to everything were so similar that Wagner had decided to prime every surface with the same copper-brown paint.

Even this was a bigger job than she had anticipated. Because of the smoothness of the surfaces, every brushstroke left an obvious trail. Wagner thought that would be a distraction, particularly if the lines of paint were deeply ridged and formed randomly, so she applied only featherweight pressure to her brush and did her best to move it in straight motions. Once the paint dried, Wagner discovered another problem: tiny bumps within the paint. On a canvas, they would be unnoticed, but on the particleboard, they were another potential distraction. Using a fine grade of sandpaper, she eliminated them. Then she repeated the painting-and-sanding cycle two more times. In the end, what she had assumed to be a two-day task had consumed a full two weeks.

The next step, the creation of a half dozen clouds that would hover above the mural's main subjects, filled the following two weeks. This work also highlighted a fundamental dilemma. In the original *Chariot of Aurora,* the clouds were more lumpy than billowy, "like sacks of potatoes," Wagner said. She had also noticed problems with the human forms. "A couple of the males have necks that look like they were put on backward. The female necks are thick and muscular, and one of them has an Adam's apple." The proportions were also off. Human hands are supposed to be about as long as their owner's face, but those in the mural were double that. "They're colossal; totally out of scale. If I replicate exactly what was there, it would look cartoonish."

Underlying all of these problems was Wagner's discomfort with the style of the original artwork. She had always been a realist painter, and *The Chariot of Aurora* was created by two of the best-known practitioners of Art Deco: Jean Dupas and Jean Dunand. "It's nothing like the work I like to do," Wagner said as she was painting one day. "I have to decide where I should be faithful to the original and where I should paint things the way they really look."

FORTY-EIGHT YEARS old, Wagner had the thoughtful manner of an academic, and her narrow-framed eyeglasses added to the impression. In fact, she never attended college. She was the middle child of five in a family of modest means—her father was a US Navy sailor, and her mother worked as a bus driver and a house cleaner—and they moved frequently. For Wagner, the main constant was her commitment to becoming an artist. She had set her course early, after her kindergarten teacher distributed crayons and asked the class to make self-portraits. Most of the results were stick figures, but Wagner's was more elaborate, and the teacher singled it out for special praise. "That was it," Wagner said. "I knew right then what I was going to be."

Wagner now lived in Palm Beach Gardens, just twenty minutes from the better-known Palm Beach but a very different kind of neighborhood. The road was made from sand and dirt, and the yellow stucco house she shared with her husband, an engineer with Florida Power & Light Company, and their three young children was surrounded not by manicured lawns but thick underbrush and cypress trees.

Nature, particularly plants, had always been Wagner's favorite subject. Her living room contained an intimate portrait of a hibiscus tree in which every detail was rendered with painstaking precision. "This is what I love," she said, "studying how each leaf and each twig is affected by light." She knew realism was often denigrated, dismissed as mere copying, and she, of course, found that offensive: "It's *not* about replicating things. It's about portraying things that photographs can't capture; things that are mostly in your head."

Despite her personal taste, Wagner had been painting large-scale works for many years. It began at Florida's Miramar High School, where she was voted the "most artistic" member of her class and where the football coach asked her to cover the locker room walls with images of his players. Prior to the financial crisis, when interior designers were eager to help their clients find one-of-a-kind ways to decorate their houses, Wagner's mural painting was in particular demand. That's how she met Linda Von Allmen, who hired Wagner to paint a bathroom ceiling with a scene straight out of the Renaissance: a sky full of cloud-straddling cherubs that had the faces of the Von Allmens' children and grandchildren. A few years later, Linda asked Wagner to create a nature scene: a representation of cherry blossoms and doves for the ceiling above the dining room of the 157-foot Trinity.

Although the Von Allmens' artistic tastes were not always in harmony with Wagner's—she hated the frolicking cherubs mural—she admired their willingness to try new ideas and to trust their own judgments, attributes that set them apart from almost all of her other clients. Their choice of *The Chariot of Aurora* was consistent with all of that. It was not something Wagner would have chosen to paint, but she understood their thinking: "They're building an impressive boat, and this will be an impressive piece of art," she said. "And Art Deco is all about glamour and opulence—the silver and gold will just jump off the wall at you."

Painting a twenty-one-foot-high mural that would stretch across three walls and be broken up by a staircase involved logistical challenges as well as careful planning, starting with determining the placement of the main figures. Wagner had decided that the sun, which would be flanked by two forms that appeared to be generating a windstorm from their mouths, would be centered on the back wall of the stairwell to become the focal point. This was a departure from her usual approach. She generally thought it was more interesting *not* to center things or organize things symmetrically, but she decided that the sun, which would sprout several triangular rays, would look odd anywhere else.

Actually rendering the sun was unexpectedly difficult. Given the straight edges of its rays, Wagner had assumed it would be mindlessly easy, a matter of "just measuring and painting; more mechanical than artistic." Once again, she had miscalculated because of the materials with which she was working. Unfamiliar with metallic paint, she did not realize how many coats it would take to produce an object that was truly golden. After the first coat, the primer paint was still visible. "It took four applications before it was solidly golden—clean and shiny," Wagner recalled.

The sheer size of the work led to other challenges. Because the sun and most of the figures spanned more than one panel, she would have liked to display all of them simultaneously. She did not have brackets that could hold the panels upright, so she arranged them on the floor—but there was not enough room for all of them. That meant she had to rearrange the panels every day or two, and because they were too heavy for Wagner to do it by herself, she had to pay assistants to help.

ON A miserably hot day in mid-July, Wagner was steaming milk for her cappuccino and preparing to start her workday. Never a morning person, the ramp-up was slow. "I always try to start working on something easy," she said. "If I start doing something complicated before my brain starts clicking, I end up doing the work twice." Just after ten o'clock, she prepared a paper plate with three small puddles of paint: silver, white, and dark brown. Sitting down in what had become her normal painting position—

hunched forward over her crossed legs so her elbows rested on her knees—she created a bird. Once it was done, she needed to move that panel from the floor and replace it with a different one that was leaning against a wall. Diane Kearley, who had been taking art classes from Wagner until she suspended them for the summer, had arrived to help.

Since walking over other panels was inevitable, they prepared for the task by distributing several freshly washed pillowcases to protect the painted surfaces from their bare feet. "It's going to take a minute for me to work my fingers underneath," Wagner said as she prepared to lift the five-foot-long panel she wanted to remove. Once both women secured their grips, they moved sideways across the room, one gentle step at a time. The replacement panel was larger, and as they moved it toward its intended destination, Wagner's back was up against a wall. As they lowered their burden, she realized there would not be enough space for her feet.

"Stop, stop!" she said. Shifting her handholds and her feet so she was no longer between the panel and the wall, her grasp was tenuous, so she said, "We have to be careful here."

The panel did not end up exactly where it needed to be, so Kearley got down on her knees and pressed its edge with the base of her palm. It still wasn't right, so Wagner said, "Let's both of us give it a push." Even then, the top surface of the new panel was not flush with that of the adjacent one. This was a problem because a female figure would extend across both of the panels, and Wagner wanted to be able to carry her brushstrokes from one to the other with as little interference as possible. They tried removing a drop cloth that was underneath a portion of one of the panels, but that didn't help either. No matter what they did, the surfaces were still not at the same level.

"Maybe the panel is warped," Wagner guessed. "Or maybe the floor isn't really flat." In any event, twenty minutes after they started the panel swapping, Wagner concluded that they could do no better.

Frustrated by how long it had taken, she said, "I'm spending at least a third of my time moving these things around."

Wagner then sat down next to the arm of the female figure. The head and neck were almost complete, and she had outlined the arm's perimeter with a thin line of chalk. As always, she began to fill out the form with the darker areas, for which she used a combination of the silver and brown paints. For the lighter sections, she used "titanium white," to which she added a small amount of silver. Her brushstrokes were long and gently swooping.

The process of endowing a flat surface with the appearance of three dimensions was something like sculpting, she explained. "Each layer creates a sense of depth. But while you're molding the paints to create layers, I also have the sense that I'm opening up the body and actually feeling the muscles and the bones with my brush."

When things were going well, Wagner fell into a groove: a one-ness with her work that eliminated distractions. It was not happening on this morning, perhaps because of the powerful thunderstorm that had moved in overhead. A radio was tuned to a station playing classical music, but the Beethoven was overwhelmed by the thunderclaps, and an announcer broke in repeatedly with weather warnings. Wagner was also preoccupied by the pressure of her deadline. "I want to bring all of these things to life," she said. "This figure needs at least a week and a half to get right. Actually, I'd like to spend twice as long as that, but I can't. If I don't stick to a somewhat loose style, it's never going to get done."

Once she was satisfied with the arm, she moved to the wrist, which she had started a few days earlier. Unhappy with her initial rendition, Wagner had asked her fourteen-year-old daughter, Cuyla, to pose a couple of days earlier. She had been a reluctant model, probably because of the unhappiness the mural had caused in Wagner's household. Several weeks earlier, she had told the children she would not have time for a family vacation this summer. Cuyla and her two brothers—Braden, who was twelve, and Ethan, ten—were generally not allowed to enter the studio. Wagner was paying Cuyla to come up with activities for her brothers, but it was clear to everyone that this would not be the best of summers. A particular low point came when Braden declared, "I know what's going on: this mural is more important than we are."

Wagner too was resentful of the time she was pouring into the project. Based on her initial belief that it would require ten or eleven forty-hour workweeks, she had accepted the $15,000 fee that Marshall had proposed; that was the amount Marshall had told Von Allmen it might cost but half what another artist had quoted. After Wagner realized it would take much longer and that she needed to pay assistants to help move panels, she called Linda Von Allmen to request a fee increase.

"I have never asked anyone for more money after agreeing to terms before," she said. "But I *really* underbid this. I should have charged you twice as much."

It was a brief conversation. Linda, with pressing financial concerns of her own, declined to pay more.

A couple of days after that, Wagner learned that the mural might be scrapped. Marshall told her the Von Allmens had put *Lady Linda* up for sale and that John Dane thought the mural was so "distinctive" that it might inhibit the marketing effort.

Marshall called a few days later to say that the Von Allmens had decided to go ahead with the mural after all, although he also mentioned that a new owner might decide to have it "painted over." For Wagner, that would be the worst possible outcome. "I want to know that my work is being enjoyed. To think that the Von Allmens might sell the boat to someone who might destroy the mural is distressing." The possibility also seemed bizarre. "If they replaced my mural with blank panels, it would look like a bland hotel. *Lady Linda* would lose its personality."

25

An Extreme Hardship

It should be warning to everyone never to go into strange places on a falling tide without a pilot.

—*FLOTSAM AND JETSAM: A YACHTSMAN'S EXPERIENCE AT SEA AND ASHORE*, THOMAS GIBSON BOWLES

STANDING ATOP a hydraulically powered lift near *Lady Linda*'s bow in late October 2011, Osly Heinandez was pulling at a two-inch-wide strip of tape several inches above what would be the yacht's waterline. The tape covered a "boot stripe," one of two decorative stripes that encircled the hull. The one he was uncovering was silver. The other was black. Tape had been placed over both stripes to prevent them from becoming besmirched by white paint when it was applied to the rest of the hull. Seeing a problem, Heinandez stopped pulling and said, "What do we have here?"

The silver paint was supposed to have a uniformly metallic sheen, but a five-inch stretch was rough and pocked. The tape had obviously lifted away some of the silver from the hull. The main challenge in restoring the stripe would be to prevent a line from forming between the area that would be repainted and the undamaged silver on either side. Heinandez began the remediation effort by using a very fine grade of dampened sandpaper to rough up the problem area as well as about three inches of unblemished paint on both sides. He then used "safe release" tape to form a precise border around the area that would be painted. He did not, however, use a vertical strip of tape to define where the sprayed paint would end at the right or the left. Instead, he rolled small amounts of the tape into two narrow cylinder shapes, with the sticky sides facing outward, and he stuck the cylinders at the ends. When the paint was sprayed, the rounded shapes would help to ensure that the amount would diminish at either end rather than stop abruptly.

"If you don't do it right," Heinandez said, "you get a line that's never going to go away."

LATER THAT day, just after dinner, Heinandez was in the living room of his house, watching his son, Jayden. Now nineteen months old, he had completed a vigorous demonstration of his running skills and had just climbed onto a precarious perch on the shoulder of a couch. Sitting nearby, Heinandez was talking about his ongoing efforts to become a legal US resident.

"The paperwork is all approved," he claimed. "We'll be going to Honduras in January or February" for an appointment at the American consulate, at which he would formally apply for a visa that would allow him to enter the United States legally. He predicted that it would be approved quickly, adding, "It's so soon that it's getting scary!"

From the nearby kitchen, Heinandez's wife popped his balloon: "The application wasn't actually accepted." Crystal explained that she and Heinandez had passed a significant hurdle—persuading the government that their marriage was real—but that the paperwork was still not yet complete and that they still had to submit almost $500 in application fees. "We also have to come up with some more money to pay our lawyer," she added. They had paid him $2,500 already and had to pay an additional $1,200 before he completed their application. Only after the monies were paid and the application was determined to be problem free would Heinandez be given an appointment at the consulate.

Heinandez did not dispute anything she said. The immigration regulations were complicated, and his understanding of them was incomplete—no better than Gale Tribble's grasp of the rules for securing disability payments. Heinandez's instinctive optimism, which sometimes got ahead of itself, was also a factor. He was desperate to put an end to the constant fear that came with his illegal status, and he was also eager to be reunited with his parents, whom he hadn't seen since leaving home six years earlier. Heinandez knew that what Crystal was saying was true—he had heard it all before—but that did not prevent him from feeling emotionally deflated. Pulling Jayden onto his lap, he wrapped his arms around his son and stared across the room.

In truth, the regulations were substantially more onerous than Crystal described. Illegal immigrants who had been in the United States for twelve months or more were required to remain outside of the country for *ten years* before they were eligible for an entry visa. The only way to get around that was to demonstrate that such a lengthy absence would cause "extreme hardship" for at least one American citizen—in Heinandez's case, potentially his wife, Jayden, or his stepchildren. While the lawyer said an exemption was likely, certainty was impossible. Individual consulates were free to define extreme hardship as they saw fit, so the process was unpredictable and potentially arbitrary. And even if Heinandez was approved for an exemption, it would not happen as quickly as he imagined. Most consulates took six to nine months to render a decision.

After Crystal finished speaking, Heinandez's gaze remained fixed on the opposite wall as he searched for something positive to say. Eventually, in a barely audible whisper, he said, *"I just know they can approve me."*

THE PAINTING of *Lady Linda*'s hull and superstructure began with the application of three coats of primer. The first two were "high-build"

epoxy-based compounds, which were intended to fill scratches made when the fairing compound had been sanded. Each of those coats was sanded also but with very fine grades of sandpaper. That was followed by the semigloss "finish primer."

The most important paintwork—the "show coats"—began after Heinandez and several coworkers erected a tent of plastic sheeting over the uppermost section of the superstructure. This was part of an elaborate effort to eradicate dust that might get caught up in the paint. Given how much of it had been created when the fairing compound was sanded and the reality that even a small amount could ruin the final finish, the precautions were elaborate. Once the tent was complete, a large fan removed air from one side of the tent while filters on the opposite side ensured that the newly introduced air was particle free. Every surface that would be painted was then wiped down: first with rags dampened with water, and then with other rags that had been sprayed with a chemical solvent, and, finally, with a knitted fabric that contained dust-gripping adhesive.

The paint that would give *Lady Linda* its snowy white complexion was a polyurethane product that cost $130 per gallon. There would be three coats, but only the first one contained pigment. The other two were totally clear, their purpose to provide a glossy finish that would be visually appealing and also offer protection from ultraviolet rays and salt. Like the fairing compound, there were two components, and combining them produced fumes that DuPont, its manufacturer, said could damage lungs and eyes and also cause liver and kidney dysfunction.

Saul Trejo, an outgoing thirty-six-year-old Mexican who played soccer with Heinandez, would operate a spray gun to apply the show coats. Prior to the shoot, he covered his head with a cotton paint sock and a full-face respirator that looked like a military gas mask, and was equipped with a carbon-based filter. He was also wearing a full-body white painting suit and latex gloves. He was wearing his own shoes, but they were completely wrapped in duct tape.

Trego would be assisted by two coworkers who were wearing the same gear. One of them would carry a pressurized two-and-a-half-gallon container of paint, the "spray pot," and the other would ensure that the hose that delivered compressed air to the pot did not become entangled or make contact with freshly painted surfaces.

The first step seemed perverse: the areas that required paint were covered and the fan was switched off. Then Trejo went into the tent and aimed the spray gun *away from* the boat. Waving the nozzle back and forth, he sent a seemingly random blitzkrieg of paint onto the inside wall of the tent. This was the final step in the dust-eradication effort, the hope being that the flying droplets of paint would collar any remaining bits of dust and lock them against the tent. After ten minutes of spraying, by which point the air had become a thick white fog, Trejo left the tent, and the fan was reactivated. Once the air cleared and the plastic that covered the yacht was removed, everything was wiped down once again with the adhesive fabric.

Painting a yacht is fundamentally no different from painting a car except that the work in auto plants is done by robots that use consistent motions to send a uniform amount of paint from a constant distance. The best yacht painters are like robots. Trejo, with his crinkly white painting suit and his taped-up shoes, did not look anything like a machine, but he handled the spray gun with machinelike consistency. The nozzle was always seven to eight inches from his target, and he moved it back and forth with a steady pendulum-like motion. The other crucial factor in his work was judging how much paint was enough. With too little, the surface would end up being perforated by little dimples that resembled those of an orange peel. If there was slightly too much, the paint would not settle evenly in the way that is required to achieve absolute smoothness and lustrous perfection. And if there was *much* too much paint, it would gather into little streams. Since there was little in the appearance of the paint to serve as a guide, getting it right was mostly a function of feel and experience.

The painting took just a half hour, far less time than the preparations that had come before. The next two coats had to be applied while the previous coat was still wet, but there had to be an hourlong pause between each application, so Trejo and his helpers stepped out of the tent and took a break before they started in on the first of the clear coats.

When they were done, *Lady Linda* was sheathed by an eggshell of plastics that was, in most places, almost a half inch thick. The outermost surface glistened like a mirror.

BECAUSE OF the dust threat, the painting of a yacht always began from the top. The underside, everything that would be underwater, came last. Since there was no need to fair those areas, the bottom was still gray and marked by welding lines.

To establish the position of the waterline, which would divide the white paint from the black that would cover the bottom, Trinity engineers used a laser to mark six locations on either side of the hull. The laser's trajectory was based on detailed calculations of what *Lady Linda* would weigh after the rest of the mechanical equipment, furniture, water, and a full load of diesel were brought on board. Not every number was knowable. For example, Heinandez and his colleagues used about five thousand gallons of faring compound, which weighed more than forty thousand pounds—but it was impossible to know how much of it had been sanded away. The engineers assumed 25 percent. They also allowed for a margin of error by setting the waterline four inches above where they thought *Lady Linda* would actually sit in the water. If they were off by an inch or two, it wouldn't matter.

The bottom was covered with several layers of paint: three coats of an anticorrosive, epoxy-based primer followed by two of a copper-based antifouling paint. The final result had the appearance of black tar. Although it was the best hull protection money could buy, it would last only two or three years. After that, *Lady Linda* would have to be removed from the water so that its underside could be painted anew.

26

Let's Roll!

Land was created to provide a place for boats to visit.

—*This Bright Land*, Brooks Atkinson

FINALLY, *Lady Linda* was ready to enter its element. After literally *years* of delay, it was, on Tuesday, November 8, 2011, to be lifted from the yard and lowered into Gulfport Lake, the adjacent body of water from which it is possible to reach the Gulf of Mexico. This did not mean the yacht was complete. Far from it. Much of the woodwork still had not been installed. Some of the onyx and marble floors had been laid down, but none of the carpets or finished ceiling panels were in place. The space that would become the galley had no appliances or cabinets. Sea trials still had to be conducted. It looked like the yacht would not actually be handed over to the Von Allmens until May or June of 2012, three years after the originally scheduled delivery date.

Still, the launch would be a major milestone and an important step forward. Once *Lady Linda* was in the water, the engines, various pumps, and other pieces of equipment could be turned on and tested, and the "mast" could be attached to the top of the fly bridge. Though it was much stubbier than the mast of a sailboat, it was too tall to be attached when the yacht was in the yard. It would provide a platform for a host of critical communications devices: radio and GPS antennas, a pair of radar arches, as well as three satellite domes that would provide navigational information, internet and phone connections, and television signals.

The preparations for the big move began Monday afternoon when Osly Heinandez climbed to the top of the scaffolding and released the plastic sheeting that still veiled the vessel. Once the plastic floated to the floor, the scaffolding itself was rolled away, and, for the first time, *Lady Linda* could be seen in full. Even in the poorly lit yard, its glossy white surfaces shimmered. The silver boot stripe revealed no imperfections. But the main impression was, quite simply, one of massiveness. The idea that the giant boat could be picked up and moved seemed absurd. Then again, now that it was possible to see how it was being supported—there were thirteen stacks of wood blocks beneath the keel and six relatively insubstantial metal braces on either side of the hull—even its stationary position seemed precarious.

After most of Trinity's workforce went home for the day, the mobile travel lift that would perform the impossible was rolled slowly toward and then over *Lady Linda* until it enveloped the yacht like a spider straddling its prey. The lift had four legs, two on either side. Each leg rested on a pair of ten-foot-tall tires. The legs were topped with a rectangular-shaped horizontal framework extending over the top of *Lady Linda* and along its sides. Everything about the powerful machine was outsized: capable of carrying 600 tons, the lift itself weighed 127 tons and had cost Trinity $1.8 million. Even the rubber tires were extraordinarily expensive: $10,000 apiece.

Sixteen steel cables hung from each side of the lift's horizontal structures. An inch and a half thick, the cables were connected to footwide straps of Kevlar. Early Monday evening, the straps from one side were buckled to those on the other and left to hang loosely a couple of feet below the hull.

IT WOULD be a week of major accomplishments for Trinity. On Thursday, its largest-ever yacht, the 242-foot *Cocoa Bean,* was scheduled to follow *Lady Linda* into the water. But the pair of launches also highlighted what was, for Trinity, a troubling reality: once these two giant yachts left the yard, only three would remain. If no new contracts were signed, that number would be reduced to two in another year. A year after that, there would be none.

While *Lady Linda* was being readied for launch, Billy Smith was discussing the facts of the yacht market in a nearby conference room. "During the three years since September 2008, we've sold exactly one yacht," he said—and at 120 feet, it was small by Trinity's recent standards. "We've experienced a perfect storm: first, the financial crisis; then, a global recession; then, the election that gave us Obama; and now, Occupy Wall Street and class warfare." And while most luxury goods businesses were recovering, there had been no improvement in the yacht-building industry. Smith blamed its exceptionalism on President Obama and the heightening political debate over income inequality. "We're in a time when no one wants to be seen spending a lot of money," he said. "You can hide the car and you can hide the jet, but yachts are just too big."

In making his point, Smith noted that the Von Allmens had recently sold a half interest in *Linda Lou* to Roger Penske, the billionaire automotive entrepreneur. It was a good result for the Von Allmens. Having failed to sell the yacht outright, they had found a way to halve their operating and maintenance costs without actually giving it up. The Von Allmens and the Penskes had even devised a way to minimize the costs of the ownership change, renaming the boat *Lime Light* so that linen, towels, and everything else that carried *LL* monograms could be retained.

But the transaction came as terrible news for Trinity because Penske had been talking to Smith about building a new yacht. "That's what's wrong with all of this political correctness about wealth distribution," Smith declared. "It's not going to hurt the rich guys. Roger

Penske isn't going to change his lifestyle. But now that he's bought half of *Linda Lou* instead of building a new yacht, there are a lot of people who won't have a job. We used to have a thousand people working here. Now we're down to six hundred twenty."

HEADA SMITH, one of Trinity's production supervisors, was responsible for orchestrating *Lady Linda*'s launch. He was a tough and sometimes ornery boss, the kind that caused workers who saw him coming to straighten their postures or, if it were possible, move out of his path. He was easy to spot: construction helmets were supposedly mandatory in the yard, but Smith wore a white cowboy hat.

Just after 6:00 a.m. on Tuesday, he was walking the length of *Lady Linda* and examining every place where there were penetrations through the hull. There were more than a dozen, each one a potential leak source. The two propeller shafts, which drove a pair of sixty-two-inch-diameter props, were the most likely source of problems. There were also holes for gauges, the drains Wayne Frierson had installed, and the intakes that would bring seawater into the engine room for cooling purposes. Near the stern were eight glass-covered apertures for lights that would make it possible to illuminate the water near the swim platform. Smith then inspected the Kevlar straps themselves, looking for tears or flaws in the stitching. Once that was accomplished, he spoke over a radio to confirm that the engineers who had come on board *Lady Linda* to ensure that various valves were locked in the closed position had left the vessel.

At 7:20 Smith held his right hand in front of his face and curled his fingers inward in come-to-me fashion. That was a signal for Rene Arguellas, who was operating the travel lift by means of a wireless control panel, to press a joystick that caused the straps to tighten slowly around the hull. With two joysticks and several buttons, the control panel did not look much different from what a child might use for a toy race car, although it did have one feature not generally found in toys: a particularly large red button at the center labeled Emergency Stop.

Once the straps made contact with the hull, Smith clenched his fist to stop the lifting. Some of his signals were easy to follow. Others were more complicated and intricate than those of an orchestra conductor. When Smith pointed his index finger toward the ground and moved it in a tight circle, that meant the cables should be lowered. If he held one finger upward just beforehand, that meant that only the cables holding the strap closest to *Lady Linda*'s bow should be lowered. Other motions meant forward or backward, right or left, fast or slow. Arguellas admitted that he did not always understand what Smith was looking to do, but he noted that there was a backup alert system: Smith was capable of producing an exceptionally loud and piercing whistle, and he did so whenever there was a problem.

At 7:32 Smith indicated that it was time to actually lift the yacht. A few seconds later, before it was evident that the yacht was rising, all but two of the piles of wood beneath the keel simultaneously collapsed. Once *Lady Linda* had risen by about a foot, Smith clenched his fist again and a pair of forklifts appeared to remove the now unneeded braces from the sides of the hull. As soon as they were taken away, a last-minute coat of bottom paint was applied to the places where the supports had been up against the hull.

Meanwhile, Smith had stationed himself in front of a panel of digital gauges that was mounted on the lift. With his arms crossed, he was watching the little red numbers that indicated how much weight was borne by the front and back halves of the lift. Maintaining a balance was crucial: if there was too much weight on either end, the lift would collapse. At the moment, the numbers said the rear section was carrying 409.5 tons and the front had 397.7 tons. While the numbers were accurate for guidance purposes, they were also misleading: they were twice as large as the actual weights, so *Lady Linda* weighed half the sum of the two, or a bit more than 400 tons.

At 7:43 Smith, who had moved directly in front of the wheels on the starboard side of the lift, shouted, "Let's roll!" Even then, as *Lady Linda* started inching toward the water, a painter continued to roll on the gunky black bottom paint. Two employees from Trinity's quality control department were also scurrying around the hull, taking photographs and videos of the sections of *Lady Linda* that would soon be underwater.

As the bow emerged from the yard just after 8:00, a dilapidated white van parked nearby. It was driven by Ricardo Gutierrez, a scuba diver who would unbuckle the Kevlar straps after *Lady Linda* was in the water. A professional diver who spent most of his time cleaning the undersides and propellers of much smaller boats, he would be paid $150 per hour for his time. By 8:18, the bow began to reach over the water as the travel lift's enormous wheels crept down the heavily reinforced concrete docks on either side of the slip into which *Lady Linda* would be placed. Twenty minutes later, Smith clenched his fist to arrest the forward motion. Pointing his right index finger toward the water, he moved it in a tight circular motion to indicate that the lowering should begin.

Five flashlight-wielding engineers were standing on a floating dock that would end up being close to the stern. When *Lady Linda*'s hull was in the water but before it was actually floating, they leaped on board to check for any incoming water. With the Trinity that had been launched before *Lady Linda,* a gusher of water entered through one of its prop shafts, and the yacht had to be lifted back out of the slip immediately. But today Smith's radio was soon crackling with good news: no leaks. Minutes later, *Lady Linda* was floating, and Gutierrez was beneath the hull unbuckling the straps.

GALE TRIBBLE was still working at Trinity, but he had been transferred to a remote part of the yard where he could not see *Lady Linda*'s journey toward the water. He still spent his days joining pieces of metal, but now he was stationed at a long workbench, and the components were much smaller. He had mixed feelings about his new role. That he no longer was required to climb stairs and crouch in awkward positions was a huge relief, but he also felt diminished and even a bit embarrassed by the smaller scale of his tasks, which he described as "piddling." As *Lady Linda* moved toward the water, he was assembling a bracket that would hold a computer screen on one of the patrol boats Trinity was building for the Kuwaiti government.

Even with his less demanding function, Tribble was unsure how long he would continue to be at Trinity. He had a new affliction, varicose veins in both of his legs, and he appeared to have lost weight. His pants were slipping off his waist even though his belt buckle was fastened as tightly as it would go. Now sixty-three, Tribble was not eligible for Medicare yet, and he could not afford to pay for his own health insurance, so the only way he could stop working was go on disability. He now understood that his own doctor could provide the information needed to file a disability claim, but he had never discussed it with him.

During his lunch break, Tribble was given the chance to go aboard *Lady Linda*. Entering the main salon, he stopped in front of the meticulously crafted piece of furniture that stood between the dining area and the rest of the space. Made from four different species of wood, the Art Deco–styled piece had gently bowed sides, a high-gloss finish, and gold-plated drawer pulls. Stunned by the craftsmanship, Tribble stood in silence until he eventually declared, "Oh, my goodness; I didn't know it was going to look like this." A few minutes later, when he saw the elaborate marble floor in Linda Von Allmen's bathroom, he was astonished anew: "This is going to be some beautiful boat. I'm so proud to be a part of it." He was also impressed by the size of things. "This bathroom is bigger than my bedroom," he said. "The bedroom is bigger than my entire house!"

Throughout his tour, Tribble repeated many of the same words over and over. As he passed through the foyer, he stopped to look at one of the columns that were being installed. The rounded shafts were sheathed with burled myrtle, a dark brown wood that had a subtle rippling effect. Running his fingers across one of them, he exclaimed, "Goodness gracious, I've never seen wood like this—this is *really* something else!"

A FEW minutes after Tribble returned to his workbench, Marty Turk, the young Azzura cabinetmaker, carried two panels of *The Chariot of Aurora* into the foyer and secured them to the wall next to the column Tribble had admired. Once the panels were in place, Turk stepped back and studied Carin Wagner's work. His appraisal was more measured than Tribble's, but he too was impressed. "It has kind of an empire feel to it," he said. "It's going to really stand out!"

Rob Shelnut, *Lady Linda*'s future captain, was also examining the mural, but he had a different kind of thought: "You know those suitcases that have the little pieces of brass in the corners? I'm thinking about what happens when a guest tries to carry one of those down the stairs."

Meanwhile, three large tanker trucks had parked next to the dock. Together they were carrying 12,500 gallons of diesel, enough to fill *Lady Linda*'s tanks to about half full. The contents of the first tanker were being pumped aboard, and Calvin Lewis, who drove the truck, was gazing up at the yacht and doing his best to take it all in.

Eventually, he blurted, "Man, oh man, what would I do?"

He said he too had a dream. He hoped to win the lottery so he could quit his job and buy a Winnebago with which he would follow the Dallas Cowboys from game to game. But now he was beginning to think more expansively.

"Can you imagine what my life would be like if that thing was mine?"

27

Chasing Dreams

To young men contemplating a voyage I'd say go.

—CAPTAIN JOSHUA SLOCUM

EVEN IN June 2012, when *Lady Linda* was finally delivered to the dock behind the Von Allmens' house, it was still unfinished. Sections of marble had to be cut and set in place, mechanical and electrical systems needed to be commissioned, furniture and artwork had to be installed. The Von Allmens' normally quiet backyard had been overtaken by shipyard-like chaos. A stone-cutting circular saw was screeching, and the dock was littered with dozens of shoes that belonged to tradesmen who were on board. There, thanks to the tarps that covered most of the floors and furniture, the interior spaces still did not look like Evan Marshall's renderings. The bridge was in particular disarray. Panels that were supposed to conceal the electronics had been removed and wires spilled out onto the floor like disemboweled guts. For good reason: the internal phone system still had not been set up, twenty-two flat-screen televisions had not been programmed, and hundreds of movies and CDs had yet to be loaded onto the entertainment system.

A deadline loomed. At five o'clock on June 19, more than forty yacht brokers would come aboard for a cocktail party. Von Allmen hoped they would be so impressed that they would go on to do one of two things: sell *Lady Linda* (for something approaching its $49.8 million asking price) or find people willing to charter it for $500,000 a week. With such lofty expectations, there could be no imperfections.

On the morning of the party, the street in front of the Von Allmens' house was lined with trucks and vans. On board, near the front of the main salon, a dent in one of the columns was being repaired by a woodworker who had earlier found a way to raise the dining room table by an inch so it could better accommodate the surrounding chairs. At the opposite end of the compartment, five large men, who all looked perplexed, were studying the curved glass door that opened to the outdoor deck. With a push of a button, it was supposed to slide back and forth almost silently, but during the trip from Gulfport, it had produced a number of unwelcome sounds. Linda Von Allmen was also in the main salon, placing a variety of decorative objects, most of them made of glass, on tabletops. During the previous couple of days, she and Marshall had gone on a shopping spree, visiting stores in Boca Raton and Palm Beach to fill any spaces that seemed wanting. The placement decisions were important—Linda confirmed each of them with masking tape and written instructions—because she was being followed by two men who were gluing the objects to the furniture so they would not topple during the transatlantic voyage that was supposed to begin the day after the party.

Marshall was standing nearby, talking on the phone and attempting to work around a potential disaster: the marble installers had not brought enough stone to complete a wall in one of the bathrooms. He had called his London office to get the name of the stone so he could try to find a local supplier who had some. Finishing the call, Marshall went to Von Allmen's bathroom to talk about the placement of the gold-plated toilet paper dispenser and a problem with the latch that was supposed to secure the shower door. Marshall then made another call to check on the status of a couple of lounge chairs that were being fabricated for the main salon. Two days earlier, Linda had rejected the pair that originally had been made for the space. "They were cumbersome and way too big," she explained. Marshall found a Fort Lauderdale furniture maker who said he would construct a set of replacement chairs in forty-eight hours.

Meanwhile, *Lady Linda*'s deckhands were squeegeeing the windows, the chef was preparing hors d'oeuvres for the party, and a tanker truck was pumping diesel through a thick hose that stretched across the Von Allmens' front and back yards. It was one of four tankers that would deliver 17,600 gallons, enough to fill *Lady Linda*'s tanks and give it sufficient range to get all the way to Monaco, where it would pick up the family that had agreed to be *Lady Linda*'s first charterers.

During the hour preceding the party, a remarkable transformation took place as contractors picked up their tools and shoes and then disappeared, carpets and furniture were uncovered, and vacuum cleaners groaned. But anxiety remained. When Teresa Manwaring, *Lady Linda*'s chief steward, saw that four large cardboard boxes still sat in the foyer outside the sky lounge, she raised her voice: "Who do these belong to? We have thirty minutes until the guests arrive!"

That was when Doug Von Allmen came on board to have his first real look at his virtually completed yacht. Given the time it had taken to plan and build, the money it had consumed, and all of the struggles, his reaction seemed strangely muted, even to someone familiar with his reticence. He seemed generally pleased by what he saw, but there was not a flicker of actual excitement and he did not want to talk about whether he had achieved his goal of creating the best-ever American-built yacht. It was impossible to know whether his reaction was just a function of his personality, the realization that he might not be *Lady Linda*'s owner for long, or something else, but when he reached the fly bridge, it became apparent that he had not stopped caring about the details. Seeing that a teak coffee table had been placed in the center of the outdoor space, he exploded: "This is not right! That table is not supposed to be there." Reaching for his cell phone, he called Marshall—who, just a couple of hours earlier, had instructed Tony Surace, whose firm built the table, to secure it in that location. Surace had done so with glue and a dozen metal pegs that fit into holes he had drilled into the teak deck.

When Surace and Marshall appeared a couple of minutes later, Von Allmen was still furious. "This really pisses me off," he told them. "We've got to move it; it gets in the way of everything!" Aware that changing the location would require removing and replacing several lengths of teak decking, Surace, looking stricken, said nothing. He hoped Marshall would do the talking, but the designer was preoccupied with trying to find a plan that would show the fly bridge. When he did so, it confirmed that the table was in the intended location. Von Allmen was not persuaded. "I can go into the house and get *my* plans," he said, "and they'll show that it's *not* supposed to be there." But seconds later, as suddenly as his anger had soared, he reversed course. "Okay, let's just leave it," he said.

A few minutes later, Von Allmen sat down on one of the sofas that faced the same coffee table. Immediately after the broker party, he and Linda planned to show several friends around the boat—they had instructed the crew to chill four bottles of Dom Perignon for their arrival—but he acknowledged that he was less than thrilled to be *Lady Linda*'s owner. It was not just about the money. In fact, a recent development had led to a dramatic improvement in his financial position: TD Bank had agreed to settle Von Allmen's lawsuit by reimbursing him for two-thirds of his losses. Von Allmen expected to recoup the rest through further litigation. It was, he said, his feelings about yachting that had changed. "The magic has worn off a bit; we have been to so many places already," he said. "I still like looking at the water and the service you get on board, but there's a bit of 'been there, done that.'"

THE FOCAL point of the party was the sky lounge. With its blue fabrics, Art Deco–styled silver doors, and a white carpet that had serpentine stripes of blue, the space was bright and elegant and, in a way that could not have been envisioned from the renderings, serene. As the brokers gathered around the bar and paid compliments to Marshall, who was perched on a stool and enjoying a glass of white wine, the chaos of the day felt like a distant memory. But even though the praise was obviously sincere, and Marshall was grateful for it, he was thinking about the future. He recognized that some of the circumstances that had come together to enable him to design *Lady Linda* and other extraordinarily large yachts were gone, and he did not believe they would come back into alignment anytime soon. "It was a red-hot market running on steroids," he said. "A lot of the money came from banks, and the money just isn't there anymore."

Then again, the modern-day era of outsized yachts was obviously not about to end. The desire of the very wealthy to build imposing boats is unalterable. So too is the elemental urge to go to sea—and the need for steady employment. And while Von Allmen's enthusiasm had waned, it was alive and well among his crew.

No one was more excited than Jerard O'Dwyer, who had helped to build *Lady Linda*'s interior as one of Azzura Marine's cabinetmakers before he became one of its deckhands. Azzura, which had lost money on its work for Trinity, had shut down a few months earlier, and O'Dwyer, a twenty-eight-year-old Australian, decided it was time for a career change. He had never spent much time on boats, and he was being paid much less than he had been as a skilled woodworker, but he hoped to work his way up through the ranks and eventually become a yacht captain. When the party began, he was wearing his new uniform—black pants and a white shirt that carried a single gold stripe on its epaulets—and greeting guests at the base of the gangplank. Looking forward to sailing across the Atlantic and seeing Europe for the first time, he declared, "This is a chance to chase my dreams."

Notes

All quotations not attributed to published sources are from personal interviews conducted by the author.

Chapter 5. Flying Above the Clouds

45 In 1982 the Americans with the largest incomes: Emmanuel Saez (University of California, Berkeley) and Thomas Pinketty (Paris School of Economics), ongoing research.

Chapter 6. Gilded Barges

54 At the Royal Yacht Squadron: John Rousmaniere, *The Luxury Yachts* (New York: Time-Life Books, 1981), 62.

55 Shortly after *North Star* arrived in England and Not long after he returned to New York: Edward J. Renehan Jr., *Commodore: The Life of Cornelius Vanderbilt* (New York: Basic Books, 2007), 187–88 and 200.

56 "Col. Astor's Steam Yacht": *New York Times,* May 21, 1899.

59 "Yachting had been a means": John Rousmaniere, *The Luxury Yachts* (New York: Time-Life Books, 1981), 99.

Chapter 11. Blinded by Thirst

103 "I grew up poor": Bob Norman, "Rise of Fort Lauderdale Attorney Scott Rothstein Has Town Talking," *New Times Broward–Palm Beach,* October 16, 2008.

104 "I don't normally do this": Nathan Koppel and Mike Esterl, "Lawyer Crashes After a Life in the Fast Lane," *Wall Street Journal,* November 14, 2009.

107 Some of the offenses: Allegations and exhibits presented in the Amended Complaint, Razorback Funding, LLC, et al versus Scott W. Rothstein et al,

Case No. 09–062943(19), Circuit Court of the 17th Judicial Circuit In and For Broward County, Florida.

108 In an email that described settlements: Exhibit B in the Amended Complaint, Razorback Funding, LLC, et al versus Scott W. Rothstein et al.

110 "We will be providing special numbers": Bob Norman, "Scott Rothstein's Emails Reveal His Mindset and Dependence on Debra Villegas," *New Times Broward–Palm Beach,* November 19, 2009.

110 In September, Rothstein told Von Allmen about another investment opportunity: the Amended Complaint, Razorback Funding, LLC, et al versus Scott W. Rothstein et al.

Chapter 12. Pulling the Trigger

116 "The great thing about a yacht": Paul Johnson, *American Spectator,* May 21, 2005.

118 Henry Ford II acquired a Feadship: "Watch the Fords Go By," *Newsweek,* April 22, 1963.

119 "There's a thrill in meeting a demand": Penn Kimball, "'Dream Town'— Large Economy Size," *New York Times Magazine,* December 14, 1952.

120 "It's absolutely excessive": Matthew Symonds, "Absolutely Excessive!" *Vanity Fair,* October 2005.

Chapter 14. Disaster

135 "It also turned out that Michael Szafranski": Affidavit of William R. Scherer, Esq., in relation to Razorback Funding et al versus Scott W. Rothstein et al. January 27, 2010.

135 "On October 31 Rothstein sent a text message": Jon Burstein, Paula McMahon, and Brittany Wallman, "Lawyer Returns As Uproar Grows" (Fort Lauderdale), *SunSentinel,* November 4, 2009.

Chapter 16. Sell Everything

150 When he spoke to Bob Norman: Bob Norman, "Large Rothstein Investor Breaks Silence," *New Times Broward–Palm Beach,* November 4, 2009.

151 "Doug wants everyone to believe": Bob Norman, "Large Rothstein Investor Breaks Silence," *New Times Broward–Palm Beach,* November 4, 2009.

153 The accountants were guilty: Razorback Funding LLC et al versus Scott W. Rothstein, et al. Circuit Court of the 17th Judicial Circuit In and For Broward County, Florida, April 20, 2010.

Chapter 19. Smooth but Unlawful

175 In an information sheet: Material safety data sheet published by DuPont's Performance Coatings division.

Acknowledgments

Writing this book required unstinting cooperation from all of its main characters. Gale Tribble, Evan Marshall, Mitch Davies, Osly Heinandez, Wayne Frierson, Carin Wagner, and Geoff Demaere allowed me to look over their shoulders as they did their work, and they also invited me into their homes—where I rewarded their hospitality by asking endless questions about their professions, their lives, and their aspirations. I am very grateful to each of them for their openness and patience, and to Doug and Linda Von Allmen, who were also generous with their time and in allowing me to follow the unexpectedly lengthy building process. I am particularly grateful to Doug for his willingness to talk candidly about his financial setbacks as well as his successes.

John Dane and Billy Smith gave me unrestricted access to their shipyard, trusting me not to get in the way or fall from scaffolding. Their patience in teaching me the details of the difficult business of building boats is also very much appreciated. When I could not be in Gulfport, I am thankful to Evan Marshall and Ingo Pfotenhauer for keeping me up to speed with regular progress reports.

Harry van Dyke supported me in every possible way throughout the project. Kathy Chetkovich, Adam Glick, David Mellgard, Mike Clifford, Robert Levy, Mark Clifford, Elisa Zachary, and Michael

Marsh read the manuscript, and each made valuable suggestions for its improvement.

John Rousmaniere led me to several excellent sources of information about the rich history of yachting—the best of which are books written by him—and he also helped me to gather a collection of historical photographs. Two talented lawyers, Jennifer Gordon and Sarah Costello, guided me through the strange intricacies of American immigration law. Jennifer Weidman, a senior counsel at Simon & Schuster, provided helpful input as the manuscript was in its final stages. Donna Burkey, a determinedly resourceful researcher at New Jersey's Morris County Library, helped me track down a number of difficult-to-find facts and publications.

Of course, none of this would have been possible if Niko Hansen and Patrick Gallagher, my longtime publishers in Germany and Australia, respectively, had not come up with the idea for the book. At Simon & Schuster, Marty Beiser and Alessandra Bastagli, my editors, as well as Daniella Wexler, Philip Bashe, and Edith Lewis, helped me to fine-tune the manuscript with uncommon care and insight. As the project moved toward publication, Priscilla Painton, Simon & Schuster's executive editor, became the book's principal champion, for which I am very grateful. Sydney Tanigawa kept everyone and everything on track during the prepublication process, even when it meant that she had to walk from Brooklyn to Simon & Schuster's Manhattan office in the aftermath of Hurricane Sandy. Kathy Robbins, my agent, provided her usual sage counsel about the words and everything else. The work of a literary agent may not be as difficult as building a large yacht, but it's probably close, and it's becoming more challenging all the time. No one does it better than Kathy.

Index

About the Author

G. BRUCE KNECHT is a former senior writer and foreign correspondent for *The Wall Street Journal* and the author of *The Proving Ground: The Inside Story of the 1998 Sydney to Hobart Race* and *Hooked: Pirates, Poaching, and the Perfect Fish.* His articles also have appeared in *The Atlantic, The New York Times Magazine, Smithsonian, National Review, Barron's, Conde Nast Traveler, SAIL,* and *Men's Journal.* Knecht received a bachelor's degree from Colgate University, earned an MBA from Harvard University, and was a Reuters Fellow at Oxford University. An avid sailor, Knecht raced across the Atlantic Ocean on *Mari-Cha IV,* the yacht that broke the one-hundred-year-old transatlantic race record. He lives in New York City.